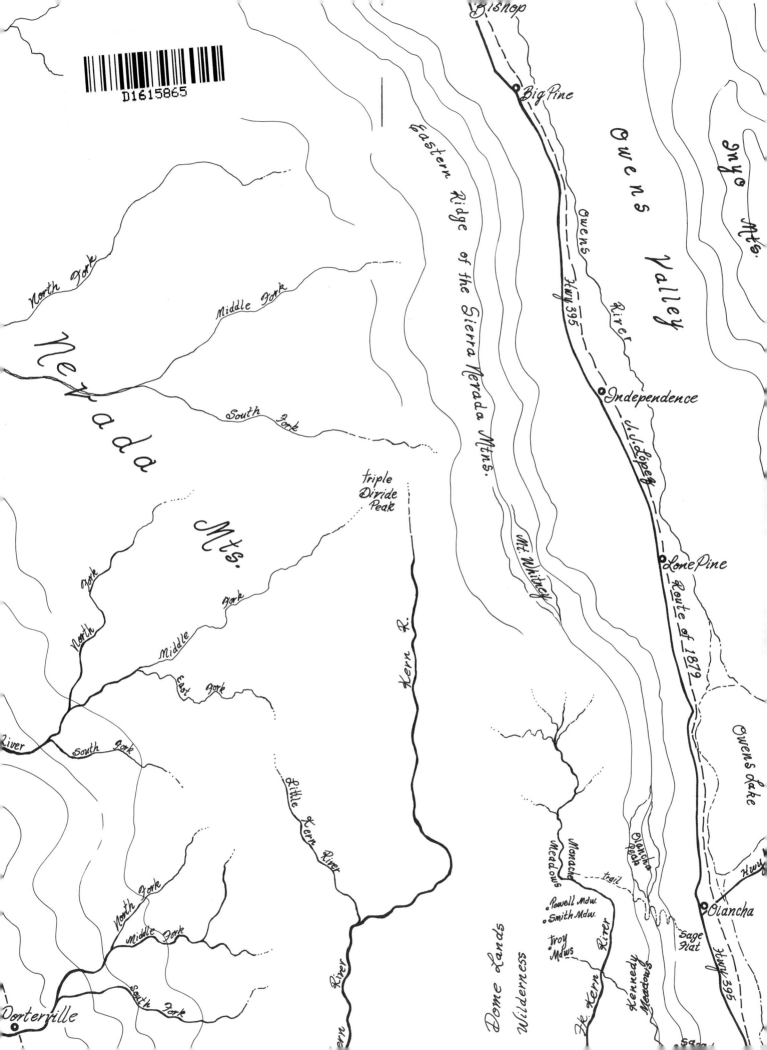

Bishop

Big Pine

Inyo Mts.

Owens Valley

Eastern Ridge of the Sierra Nevada Mts.

North Fork

Middle Fork

Nevada

South Fork

Mts.

Triple Divide Peak

Fork

North

Middle

East Fork

River

South Fork

Little Kern River

Kern R.

Owens River

Hwy 395

Independence

L. J. López

Lone Pine

Route of 1879

Mt. Whitney

Owens Lake

North Fork

Middle Fork

South Fork

Porterville

River

Monache Meadows

Powell Mdw.

Smith Mdw.

Troy Mdws

The Kern River

Kennedy Meadows

Olancho Peak

trail

Olancha

Sage Flat

Hwy

Dome Lands Wilderness

Hwy 395

MARYLOU
SLINKARD
© 1986

Bob Powers
"COWBOY COUNTRY"

# Cowboy Country

## by Bob Powers

THE ARTHUR H. CLARK COMPANY
Spokane, Washington                    2000

*Dedicated to the cattlemen, the artists who deal not with the media of oils or clay, but with the "green pastures and still waters" and the living flesh and blood of animals.*

# Table of Contents

# Acknowledgments

The author wishes to acknowledge, with heartfelt thanks, the contributions of the following people: Bill and Mona Carver, for their help in obtaining pictures of the Glennville cattlemen; Ethel Olivas, Ada Brown and Joy Anderson of Lone Pine for locating photos of the Inyo County cattlemen; Bill Horst for his superb maps; M.E. Ensminger B.S., M.A., Ph.D., distinguished professor and author of *Beef Cattle Science,* for his help to this author and thousands of other cattlemen by his painstaking work in the beef cattle field. Also, thanks to many cowboy friends, such as Andy Charlton, Clifford Cross and Wink Chappell for the many hours spent talking about old-time cowboying. Thanks also to Joe Herin for the pictures of the ZX Ranch, and to Casey Christie for his fine photos.

# Foreword

The cattle business and cowboys have been fact and tradition in my family for the past four generations. In 1852, one of my great-grandfathers, John W. Powers, brought "a large drove of cattle" from Missouri and settled in northern California where he raised his family. Another great-grandfather, Thomas H. Smith, was listed as a stockraiser when he settled in the Kern River Valley in 1861. Down through the years, my grandfather, James H. Powers, and my dad, Marvin P. Powers, also followed this same business in this same area. With that background, I guess it was only natural that from the time I was given my first cowboy hat and a pair of red angora chaps at the age of seven, I would grow up wanting to be a cowboy.

I stayed on the home ranch until I was twenty-eight, and I have spent many days since working cattle. However, I still don't consider myself to be what would be classified as a top-hand. The best way I can think of to get myself in trouble is to set myself up as an authority on the cattle business, but because I have been so closely associated with it for so many years, I have a desire to record some stories and impressions on this subject.

From the years 1952 to 1982, the cattle business changed more than it had in the previous one hundred years. During these years, I didn't have much to do with the day-to-day working of a cattle ranch. We had sold our family ranch in 1952, and while I was associated to some degree with the cattle industry through my job as Range Officer for the U.S. Forest Service, I didn't have the close contact I had enjoyed for the first part of my life.

After I retired from the Forest Service, I took a job in 1981 as ranch manager for one of the ranches on my home range. I feel that because I had been away from the business for some years, I was able to look more objectively at the changes that needed to be made. I was able to recommend methods such as crossbreeding and culling cows who didn't wean a big calf every year. I was able to put aside some traditional methods and take advantage of the world of information available on what is called "the new cattle industry." Although I retired after just five years, I saw a marked improvement in the pounds of beef shipped to market.

There is a crowd of old-timers who are real experts on this subject. However, they don't write books, and in a lot of cases, would rather not discuss their plan of operation, prices received for cattle, etc., as they feel it is the same as discussing their bank account. Even though it might seem presumptuous on my part to tackle this project, I hope what is written will be taken as just "one man's opinion," and that my love for cowboying, the cattle business, and everything associated with it, will overshadow my lack of expertise.

# Cowboy Country

# Cattlemen and Cowboys

Cattlemen have been the forerunners of civilization since the days when Abraham and Lot pastured their cattle along the Jordan River. Although the handling of cattle is one of the oldest pursuits of mankind, it wasn't until about 120 years ago that the term "cowboy" was used for the men who worked in this profession. It was first used for the boys who had just previously served in the Civil War and were working cattle in Texas between 1865 and 1870. Whether these men were called vaqueros, drovers, cow-punchers,* or the most common term, cowboys, this group of individuals have contributed more to the myths and literature of the world than any other profession in history.

Still, the cowboy today is as hard to stereotype as he was 100 years ago. They come in all shapes and sizes and have temperaments that range from one extreme to the other. There are those who dress "fit to kill" even in dusty, hard-working situations, and others who don't care that much about how they look as long as what they wear is comfortable and serviceable. There are cowboys who are at home only in a rodeo arena, those who have worked mostly in feed lots or pasture situations, and those who have worked most of their lives on the open range. I would be the first to say, however, that there have been plenty of cowboys around in each generation for the past seventy-five years who could make top hand in any of these areas.

Where do these cowboys come from? From all walks of life. However, I think one is more apt to answer this calling if he or she is born into the profession. The Mexican people have a saying which, when loosely translated, is "a cowboy is made when he is a slobbering babe, not after he is grow-

ing a beard." Many in the cattle profession use the saying, "Cowboys are born and not made." The cowboys I think of when I hear that statement are my neighbors, Buckshot and Tippi Tipton. They were raised on the Tejon Ranch, one of the largest ranches in California. Their father and grandfather also worked there, and they grew up living and breathing horses and cattle. Their father, Tipton, Sr., still holds down a line camp in Kelso Canyon, twenty-two miles from the nearest store and telephone. People who have grown up in association

Burel Mulkey, the World Champion All Around Cowboy of 1938. In 1968 Mulkey's name was entered into the Rodeo Hall of Fame.

* A name first given to the cow hands who used long poles to crowd steers into railroad cars in Abilene in the late 1860's.

15

Franky Schneider, the World Champion Bull Rider of 1933 and 1934. He was also the World Champion Bareback Rider of 1935. Franky was a cowboy and rancher all his life. He married a Kern River Valley girl, Eleanor Silicz, better known as Sis.

with the cattle business all their early lives are more apt to be what are classed as top hands.

I would venture to say that a cowboy can't be bought. If he likes the outfit and the way it is run, many times he will stay for years. In some cases he will work most of his life for one ranch.

The wages they receive are often surprisingly low compared with what they would be for other tradesmen who have spent a comparable period of time learning their profession. Because of this, many cowboys choose to work on cow outfits because they are attracted to this type of life and not to make big money. If the management is fairly easy to get along with, the working conditions passable, they will stay because they wouldn't be happy in any other occupation. On most ranches there is no retirement plan for the employees. Very few cowboys worry too much about this; they just plan to ride until the end of their days. This is what my uncle, Jack Powers, did. After sixty years on horseback, he had a heart attack while working cattle and fell off his horse with his lass rope still in his hand.

The rancher is usually made up of the same material as the cowboy. They really have to love ranching or they would never risk their money in something as unpredictable as the cattle business. Unlike the cowboy, if sledding gets rough the rancher can't saddle up and ride on to another ranch. Usually, if they decide to sell out, there is no

Burel Mulkey, the World Champion Saddle Bronk Rider of 1937. Burel married Marion (Mernie) Silicz. He was a cowboy in the Kern River Valley until the time of his death.

16

Tip Tipton, Sr. with his sons, Buckshot (left) and Tippy. (Photo by Casey Christie).

way they can get back their investment in time and money. At times a small ranch owner receives even less per hour than the hired cowboy, especially if you add the hours the rest of his family contributes without monetary compensation. It is hard to understand why a man or woman would spend his or her whole life working for what seems such minimal rewards, but it would be hard to find many ranchers who would trade their job for any other, even for ten times the money.

Most ranchers I have known ride right along with their cowboys. In camp they do their share of the chores, whether it is cooking, washing dishes, or bringing in fire wood. Most of them love to work with horses and cattle every bit as much as their cowboy counterparts. While the owner of a ranch has the dubious honor of being the boss, he also is the one who lies awake at night worrying about how the bills will be paid. If a rancher has been in business for years and is still surviving, it means he must be doing something right. From my standpoint, success in the cattle business is about forty percent luck (a good feed year) and sixty percent

knowledge of the business (at least for those in my area who depend on rain to grow their feed).

The rancher does have the option to take a day off when he wants to, but many of them only take days off for medical reasons or to go on a "busman's holiday" (cattlemen's conventions and other ranch-related business).

There is a lot of overlap between the two groups, ranchers and cowboys. Many cowboys also run small bunches of cattle for themselves, even though not many of them own their own land. All in all, there is a lot of camaraderie between the two groups and, as I don't know how to part them, I hope they won't mind if I seem to lump them together in pictures and text.

Cattle have been grazing on open range in and around the Kern River Valley for over one hundred years. But, before making an attempt to trace the changes brought about in this valley over the last century, it might be best to give a little background on the origin and domestication of the beef animal as we know it today.

The majority of the cattle found in the world

today are believed to be the descendants of the massive Aurochs, hunted in the forests of central Europe in the Old Stone Age. The first indication of these bison appear in rock drawings made by the Paleolithic men 17,000 to 20,000 years ago. Some of these drawings were found painted on the walls of a cave in what is now southern France near Lascaux, France. These cattle were not domesticated until the Neolithic age in Asia Minor. During this period, man changed from a hunter of cattle to a herder of cattle. I think even today some cattlemen spend more time hunting their cattle than they do herding them.

The Aurochs approached tremendous size. This has been proven by complete skeletons, measuring six to seven feet at the withers, that have been found in bogs. While the earliest drawings were of the Bos taurus, the blood of most of the early cattle is thought to be a combination of the Bos taurus and Poas indicus. The Bos taurus, which came from the more temperate zones, seem to be a mixture of the Aurochs (Bos premingenuis) and the Celtic shorthorn (Bos longifosus). The Bos indicus belong to the Zebu (Brahman) group.

When cattle were first domesticated they were probably used for draft purposes, but it wasn't long before they were used for meat and milk by nomadic people who lived mainly on the products of their herds. The Bible, as well as other historic literature, referred to the milk cows, the fatted calf, and also the stall fed ox.

The first person to lead the way in improving beef cattle was Robert Bakewell (1726-1795) of Dishley, England. Most of Bakewell's efforts were directed to trying to perfect the English Longhorn, common to the Tees River area. The weights alone of the cattle sold in the famous Smithfield Market point out how Bakewell's efforts improved the beef breed by selecting the outstanding animals for breeding purposes. In 1710, beeves averaged 370 pounds, but by 1795 they averaged 800 pounds. He truly put a firm foundation under future methods of improving livestock. At the time Bakewell's English Longhorns were popular, they were probably the only distinct breed of cattle that existed in England. In the year 1783, the celebrated Shorthorn bull Hubback was only six years old, and the Hereford and Devon breeds were purely local.

Cattle are not native to the Western Hemisphere. In 1498, the Spanish Crown established a royal farm on Santo Domingo in the West Indies. Besides horses of the Arab and Barb strain, Columbus also brought cattle of the Andalusian breed. These animals were a tough breed, predominately black in color with needle-sharp horns. They multiplied at such a fast rate that not only were they furnishing all the meat needed for the colonists, but there were excess numbers to establish the breed in other locations. In 1521, Gregorio de Villelobos took six of these Andalusian heifers and a bull from Santo Domingo to Vera Cruz, Mexico. Soon after, Cortez established a ranch in Oaxaca Valley in Mexico, with many others quickly following his example.

It was in Mexico that these descendants of Asia's nomadic herdsmen came to be the forerunners of the American cowboy. With their long-shanked, big roweled spurs and their long braided rawhide reatas, the Vaqueros in connection with the first horses and the first domesticated cows did more to settle the New World than anything else. By 1540, there were a number of going ranches strung the length of both the east and west coasts of Mexico. In that year, Coronado became the first American trail driver when he drove five hundred cattle and sixteen hundred horses and mules from Culican, Mexico, to Zuni, Arizona. Also, Luis de Carabojal started his ranch at Cerralvo just south of the Texas border, In 1555, Onate founded his ranch in Santa Fe and in 1565, Pedro Mendenez Avillas became Florida's first cowman.

The first arrival of cattle to the east coast was in 1609 when colonists from England brought the first few over. Other English importations soon followed with Governor Edward Winslow bringing a notable number in 1623. As colonists came to the shores of New England they brought with them the type of cattle they were accustomed to in their mother country. Although they might have differed in color and size, their basic similarity was their ruggedness and their ability to work under the yoke. At first the colonists valued their cattle mostly as work animals rather than for milk, butter and hides, with little value being placed on their meat. This was because wild game was so plentiful. Cattle were so necessary for draft purposes that in some early-day town meetings ordinances were passed making it a criminal offense to slaughter a work-ox until after he had passed his useful work age, which was seven or more years.

The requirements for these work oxen were that they had long lean legs, with lean muscular bodies and heavy heads and necks. Oxen of this type were needed for clearing the forests and plowing the rugged new land and also for hauling their produce over rough roads to seaport markets. All during the colonial period the American farmers had let their animals shift for themselves. Even in the winter, food and shelter was rarely provided. As more cattle were acquired they had to be taken farther from town to find enough feed. They were taken care of by a paid "cowkeeper," which might be counted as one of the first cowboys in the Western Hemisphere. They would be taken out in the morning and returned to the village in the evening.

Even in the early days the bull was considered very important to the village economy. The animals to be kept for sires would be picked by the town fathers and if any of the citizens owned a bull of superior quality, they would be paid an approved service fee on a per head basis.

As time passed, the colonists realized the need for blooded stock to improve their cattle. These early stockmen could draw from the improved animals now in Europe, especially from England. One instance of this was in 1783 when three farmers by the names of Patton, Goff and Ringold went to England for the best cattle that could be obtained. In this way the stock in New England were gradually improved.

Beginning in 1769, cattle were brought over from Spain for work purposes in connection with a chain of Christian missions established by the Spaniards among the Indians of the New World. This string of missions extended from the east coast of Mexico up the Rio Grande. From there they extended across the mountains to the Pacific Coast. There were abundant feed and water in this vicinity, and by 1833, the Spanish Priests estimated their missions owned about 424,000 head. Many of these animals were running loose in a semi-wild state.

A description of how wild these cattle became is found in the diary of Zenas Leonard when he was in California with Joseph Walker in 1833.*

"On the evening of the 22nd November we encamped at some rough hills near a small creek. In this neighborhood there are great number of these hills, all of which are well covered with excellent timber, and abounding with all kinds of game except buffalo. The most of our company had become nearly barefooted for want of moccasins, as we had wore out everything of the kind in traveling from the Rocky Mountains—and, as winter was approaching, and no one knowing what kind of a

reception we would meet with among the Spaniards, it was advised that we should tarry here and provide ourselves with an abundant winter supply of shoes. Accordingly, our hunters were despatched to scour these hills for the purpose of getting hides to make moccasins, etc., when we would be at leisure. In the evening the hunters all returned to camp, with the tongues of 93 deer and some of the hides, and also of some wild-cattle, which are likewise very numerous. They brought the tongues in order to show the number each man had killed. The wild cattle are very timorous, keeping hid pretty much all day and feed at night. They are much wilder than deer, elk, etc. Our hunters brought in some of the choice parts of the cattle they had killed, which was quite fat beef, but it was much inferior to the meat of the buffalo of the Rocky Mountains. These cattle incline much to rough and hilly parts of the country, owing, it is supposed, to the Spaniards and Indians hunting them when found in the plains.

"23d. This morning we directed our course across these hills. On arriving at the foot of the hills on the south side, we found one of the horns of these cattle which measured three and one-half feet on the outside or bend, and one foot in circumference at the root or thickest part."

On April 11, 1822, California fell under the imperial flag of Mexico and it wasn't long until the Mexican government was issuing land grants to its citizens. By 1826, the missions were supplying foundation stock for ranchos started on these grants. With an abundance of feed and better management than that provided by the missions, the cattle owned by the ranchos outnumbered those owned by the missions.

In the early years, the chief market for the cattle on these ranchos was for hides and tallow, as there wasn't that much demand for the meat. Starting in 1800, New England traders sailing around the Horn established a brisk business, first with the Spanish and then Mexican ranchers. These ships that sailed around the Horn were almost equivalent to the modern-day department store. Anchored off the California coast, they traded hides and tallow for goods not available in California in those days. Hides became known as "California banknotes." In trade, they were worth two to five dollars each, but in cold hard cash, only about $1.50 each. Tallow was traded at $2.50 for 25 pounds with payment usually taken half in trade and half in hard money.

A good description of this hide and tallow trade

*This account was published in a book by the name of *Adventures of Zenas Leonard, Fur Trader,* edited by John C. Ewers, University of Oklahoma Press.

and how the animals were killed is found in the book, *Two Years Before the Mast* by Richard Dana.* Dana was on the California coast in 1835. The following was taken from this book:

"The principal part of their hides are sold to U.S. vessels trading on the coast. When a trading vessel anchors on the coast for the purpose of trading, the news is spread over the whole country like wildfire. The owners of cattle, who are of the wealthier class, collect together all the poorer Spaniards and Indians for the purpose of catching and butchering the cattle, in order to get their hides. This is the commencement of their sporting season. They are all mounted on their fleetest horses, and on these occasions the hunters go in pairs, one provided with a noose and the other with a spear or lance, which is used in cutting the sinews of the animal's hind legs after it is noosed, which causes it to fall to the ground, after which they are easily despatched. After they strip off the hides and take out the tallow, and sometimes the choice part of the meat, the remainder of the carcass is left on the ground to be devoured by the wolves. The hides are then stretched out on the ground, and the tallow moulded into large cakes. As a compensation for their labor, the butchers, or hunters, receive one-third of all the tallow they can collect. When the vessel is about ready to leave the coast, the hides and tallow which has been collected is conveyed to the beach, where the hides are sold at $1.50 apiece, and the tallow at four cents per pound.

"The greater part of this cargo is paid for in merchandise at high prices, but which is as valuable here as money itself, and much more useful. A vessel loaded with hides and tallow from this coast is of the greatest value, and has afforded an easy path to wealth for many of the American merchants."

Another cash crop for the Mexican citizens in California was the sale of mules. How this was done is found in Josiah Gregg's *Commerce of the Prairies,* reprinted in 1954 by University of Oklahoma Press. It tells how, "the dry season is occupied by the inhabitants in gathering the mules into large droves and driving them off to the market at Santa Fe, a distance of twelve or fourteen hundred miles from this part of the coast, through a wild and desert country. Here they meet with ready sale at a profitable price from the traders of Missouri who repair to Santa Fe annually for that purpose.

*This account was also published in a book by the name of *Adventures of Zenas Leonard, Fur Trader,* edited by John C. Ewers, University of Oklahoma Press.

These traders are generally well supplied with merchandise which they exchange at Santa Fe for gold and silver, and with these California traders for mules and Spanish hides. The price of a mule at Santa Fe is generally from six to ten dollars. Merchandise is sold at a great advance, particularly silks, jewelry, and groceries."

During this same period, a memorable cattle drive took place from California to the Willamette Valley in Oregon. This wasn't made by a Spanish rancher, but by the former fur trapper, Ewing Young. Young, who first entered California in 1829, later settled in the Willamette Valley of Oregon in 1837. At that time, there were only twenty-three head of cattle there, which were owned by the Hudson Bay Company. These were the only cattle in that part of Oregon, and were being kept only for breeding, trying to build up a larger herd.

Young had seen the great herds in California, so he formulated a plan to buy a herd in California and drive them to Oregon. Young purchased 800 head of cattle from the San Jose Mission and the San Francisco Solano Mission for $3.00 per head. With nine men to assist him, he headed north. This proved to be one of the most difficult drives ever recorded. He didn't call his men "cowboys," but I'd be willing to bet when they arrived in the Willamette Valley nine months later they understood what cowboying was all about. They had been pounded by storms, almost washed away by flooding streams, and brought almost to a standstill at times by thick forests and underbrush. Twice, Young had to hold his pistol to his men to keep them from mutiny.

At the end of the trip there were only 632 left of the original 800 head. After they were sold for $7.69 per head, the men were paid a dollar a day. This amounted to $2,430 and just covered his purchase price. All Ewing Young received was a lot of experience.

Cattle raising spread out from the coast of California, but it wasn't until 1842 that it reached as far inland as the San Joaquin Valley, in what is now known as Kern County.

On July 14, 1842, California Governor Juan Balvarado issued to Jose Antonio Dominguez, a canyon known as the San Emigdo, which was four square leagues of land. This grant was stocked with cattle by Dominguez. He died during the winter of 1843-44, and because the rancho was so isolated and the Indians were causing trouble, his widow removed the cattle and abandoned the land. In

1846, when California came under the domination of the United States, the validity of early Mexican grants was upheld, and in 1852 the 17,706 acre San Emigdo tract was sold to the well-known frontiersman, John C. Fremont. After several owners, it eventually became part of the Kern County Land Company.

The next grant issued in this area was in 1843 for 22,178 acres. This grant was named Rancho Castaic, with the western boundary near Uvas Canyon. Jose Maria Covarrubias, from Santa Barbara, put cattle on this land soon after he obtained title. Also in 1843, Jose Antonio Aguirre and Ignacio de Valle, who both lived in Los Angeles, were granted the 97,612 acre tract named Rancho El Tejon. This tract extended from Agua Caliente Creek south to the Tehachapi Mountains. They hired Indians to build corrals and take care of the livestock.

In 1846, Francisco Lopez, Vicente Bottiler and Luis Jordon, all of Los Angeles, were granted 26,625 acres they called Rancho Los Alamos y Agua Caliente. This rancho was located east of Rancho Castaic. When Lopez moved livestock to the rancho, his vaqueros refused to stay because of the hostility of the Indians. Also in 1846, a 48,799 acre tract became Rancho La Liebre, which was granted to Jose Maria Flores who lived in Los Angeles. It was located on the southern side of the Tehachapi Mountains and along the western edge of Antelope Valley. In partnership with Francisco Garcia Flores, he placed livestock on Rancho La Liebre in 1848. This is the only grant of the above mentioned that lay partially in Los Angeles County. The rest were all in what later was to become Kern County, and all became part of the Tejon Ranch.

In 1846, war broke out between the United States and Mexico. Because they did not want to be in this isolated area during war time, the owners of most of the Tehachapi Mountain Ranchos removed their livestock, and others left their ranchos in charge of Indian employees. In 1848, the war with Mexico ended with the signing of the Treaty of Guadalupe Hidalgo, and California became a United States Territory. The Mexican ranchos had not been occupied very long by these new owners, but the validity titles of all of their grants were upheld by judicial action. These grants were eventually purchased by American ranchers.

After gold was discovered in California in 1848, it wasn't many years before gold seekers had spread throughout what would later be Kern County. They were disturbing the way of life of the native Indian and driving out the game that their livelihood de-

pended on. Because of this, the Indians started plundering stock south of the Tehachapi Mountains and stealing horses, not only to eat, but also to ride. The Los Angeles-Stockton Road ran through the San Joaquin Valley and the Indians were also terrorizing the travelers along this early road.

California was admitted to the Union on September 9, 1850. Twenty-seven counties were created and one of these, the enormous Mariposa County, contained what would later be Kern County.

In 1851, the United States government opened treaty negotiations with eleven tribes in the area. In 1852, Edward F. Beale, a veteran of the war between the United States and Mexico, was appointed Superintendent of Indian Affairs in California by President Millard Fillmore. Federal jurisdiction was established over the tribes, and the Indians agreed to give up certain areas with the assurance that the government would set aside reservation lands. The commissioners also agreed to furnish supplies for the Indians. A suitable location for a reservation could not be decided on. The miners didn't want the reservation in the mountains, and the settlers in the valley felt it would curtail their ranching operations there. They felt the commission was being too generous. Since no headway was being made in setting aside an Indian Reservation, Lieutenant Beale suggested an alternate plan. He suggested, as wards of the federal government, the Indians be placed on military reservations, and this reservation could be relocated if the pressure from the frontiersmen made it necessary. In 1853, Congress authorized the creation of these reservations, and Beale arrived to look for a site for one in the Tejon area. Lieutenant Robert S. Williamson was in the area with his railroad survey party and he recommended Tejon Canyon as a suitable location. The reservation was named the Sebastian Reservation after William K. Sebastian. He was a United States Senator from Arkansas, and he had been a firm supporter of the plans of Lieutenant Beale. In 1854, Lieutenant Beale reported there were twenty-five hundred Indians living on the Sebastian Reservation.

In 1854, a United States Army post, Fort Tejon, was established some fifteen miles southwest of Uvas Canyon.* Fort Tejon was the chief military center between Los Angeles and Fort Miller†, in northern California. Most of the officers and also many of the enlisted men were seasoned Indian

*Cañada de las Uvas (Grapevine Canyon).
†Millerton Lake in Fresno County now covers this site.

fighters and frontiersmen, and many were veterans of the Mexican War. Many officers who would make names for themselves in the War between the States started out at Fort Tejon. Men such as Grant, Sherman, and Stonemen. When the Civil War began, troops were taken from Fort Tejon, and when the last troops left on June 15, 1861, the Fort was abandoned as a military operation.

Much of the property that comprised the Sebastian Reservation was made up of land grants issued by the Mexican Government, but not much attention was paid to this until 1863, when the new owner of these grants said he had plans to develop a ranch on the property. This new owner was none other than General Edward F. Beale, who had lost his job as Superintendent of Indian Affairs for California nine years earlier. By the early 1860's, Beale had been appointed Surveyor General of California by President Lincoln. While Beale held this office, he bought the La Liebre grant, the Castaic grant, the original Tejon grant, and the Los Alamos grant, a total of 195,000 acres. He purchased them for various prices, some as low as fifty cents per acre. When General Beale was on a trip to Washington, he told President Lincoln of his purchases and the President is said to have remarked, "Beale, you truly are master of all you survey."

Known first as Beale, Baker and Company, for quite a few years Beale ran sheep on his ranch in pastures with Colonel R. M. Baker. They had, at one time, 100,000 head of sheep on the ranch, tended by 50 Indian herders.

When General Beale first stocked the ranch with sheep in 1863, he placed Francisco (Chico) Acuna in charge of them. Chico was trained in the vast desert country of Mexico in the state of Sonora. His early training in this arid, rough land made the problems that came up on the Tejon Ranch seem fairly simple. Men that knew Chico Acuna listed him as one of the most able stock men to ever run cattle or sheep in California. Not only with stock, but he also had a reputation for handling men that was hard to beat. He worked for General Beale for twenty-six years. During the last nine years of his employment, he had a great influence on Don Jose Jesus Lopez, who was to take over as the next majordomo (boss) for the Tejon Ranch when Chico retired.

J. J. Lopez, as everyone called him, was put in charge of the sheep on the Tejon Ranch by General Beale in 1874, and at that time, the ranch was running about 100,000 head of sheep. Lopez had been

Mary and Jose J. Lopez. Mrs. Lopez was the daughter of James and Jennie Winter. Mr. and Mrs. Lopez had **one daughter, Pearl Meacham, living in Bakersfield in 1987. Mrs. Lopez' brothers herded sheep on the Tejon Ranch, and several generations of the Lopez family** cowboyed there.

in charge of the sheep only three years when the country was hit with a severe drought. While many of the stockmen in the San Joaquin Valley lost most of their livestock during this drought, the Tejon Ranch was able to save all of their stock. At this time, they had 10,000 head of cattle and 68,000 head of sheep on the ranch. The reason the Tejon Ranch was able to save their stock was because they had access to the swampy areas around most of Kern Lake. Also, the upper part of the Tejon Ranch hadn't been grazed the year before and there was a lot of dry feed left.

The following winter, 1878-79, there was also very limited rain, so General Beale decided to start cutting down on the number of sheep kept on the ranch. At this time, they considered changing the ranch operation from sheep to raising only cattle. During this period, sheep were worth only from one dollar to one dollar and fifty cents per head. However, there was no demand for them as the market was distressed because others were trying to dispose of their sheep that they had no feed for. Because of this, it was decided that a series of large droves would be taken up through the Mojave Desert and on north into the Owens River Valley, fattening them as they went. Near Bishop, they would turn through the Sierra Mountain Range, coming out into the Sacramento Valley. They would be met there by Senator Boggs, who was one of the lessors of the Tejon Ranch, and he would sell the sheep.

J. J. Lopez organized the first drove, and on May 15th, 1879, he left Ranch Liebre, Headquarters on the Tejon Ranch, with 16,000 head of sheep. He took with him a total of twenty-two men. The sheep were split into eight bands of 2,000 each with two drovers in charge of each band. They took with them a chuck wagon and a light army ambulance that had been used years before at Fort Tejon. They carried barrels of water for the horses, cooking and drinking. Besides their food, bedding, and cooking gear, they also carried a little hay.

The weather was hot when they left and crossed the Antelope Valley. About three days out at Oak Creek, a snowstorm caught them and they had to lay over three days. From Oak Creek, they continued to Desert Springs and the next night camped at Red Rock Canyon. The rest of the trip as far as Bishop was fairly uneventful and Lopez was pleased at the way the sheep were gaining weight on the good feed. This feed was so good because there hadn't been any livestock grazing here at this time. When they arrived in Bishop, there was a letter waiting for Lopez changing his orders. He was to turn east with the sheep and take them to a town called Piache, which was near the west boundary of Utah. The letter said sheep were bringing a good price there and that Senator Boggs would meet them there to sell the sheep.

This route would take them across some of the most desolate desert country in the west and everybody was very discouraged. The perils of trying to

Tejon Ranch branding crew in the early 1940's. Archie Winter, Sr.; Charlie Wilbanks, the cook; Tony Araujo, Walt Thompson, and John Gomez, with only one leg, but who could cowboy with the best of them.

drive sheep across this section of the country were well known, especially the Deep Springs Valley in Nevada. While driving through this area in 1875, Harry Quinn from Delano had saved only 2,200 head out of his drove of 22,000, and two years later, John Baker lost 13,000 head from his band of 22,000. Both of these men were old hands at handling sheep in the desert. What Lopez and his men were attempting seemed impossible. For one stretch of 130 miles they had no water for their sheep and they had to travel eighteen days without water. They did lose 5,000 head, but felt they were

The Tejon ranch crew eats in the shade of the giant oaks. From left: Tip Tipton, Sr., Red Noble, Frank Apodaca, Kenneth Winsor, unidentified. Front - Harry Malone, unidentified, John Gomez.

Tejon Ranch in 1939. Tip Tipton, Sr. is on the left and Henry Gross on the right.

horse gear for a saddle horse he led behind the buckboard. Though J. J. Lopez retired in 1926, when he died in 1939 he was still active as a consulting cattle boss after sixty-five years on the Tejon Ranch.

Antonie (Tony) Araujo was born on the Cummings Ranch near Tehachapi. He was the grandson of Ramon Araujo, who arrived in Kern County in 1842. Tony's mother died when he was very young and he was placed in an orphanage until he was seven. After being placed in the care of various aunts and uncles, in 1900, when he was eleven years old, he came to the Tejon Ranch to live with his father. He started living with the J. J. Lopez family at the age of fourteen, and when he was nineteen, he started riding full time for the Tejon Ranch.

Tony had an excellent teacher in J. J. Lopez, and in 1926, when Lopez went into semi-retirement, he was appointed cattle superintendent, a position he held for thirty-five years. During that time, he was directly responsible for 20,000 head of cattle ranging over some 350,000 acres.

In 1976, the Kern County Cattlemen honored Tony. Harold Thurber, who made the presentation, described Tony as, "One of the great Vaqueros, one we admire as a friend, cowman, horseman, roper, craftsman, and above all, a true gentlemen." In 1981, just a year before he died, Tony was voted into the Cowboy Hall of Fame in Oklahoma City, a well deserved honor.

Also inducted into the Cowboy Hall of Fame at the same time was Lou Rochford. Rochford, who was eighty-four at the time, became resident manager of the Tejon Company in 1943, and eventually moved upwards in the Tejon Company until he finally became Chairman of the Board. Rochford was recognized for his leadership in herd improvement through breed record keeping. He retired from active duty in 1963, but remained as a consultant to the Tejon Ranch for many years. In 1987, Matt Echeverria was ranch manager and George Noblia was in charge of the cattle operation.

lucky to get out with their lives. At this time, their orders were changed again, and they still had to travel 1,000 miles to their new destination of Green River, Wyoming. However, the worst part of the trip was over. A more complete account of this historic drive can be found in *Saga of Rancho El Tejon,* by Frank Latta, and makes very interesting reading.

On this drive, J. J. Lopez convinced General Beale of his ability to handle men and livestock. In 1885, Lopez was placed in charge of the entire stock operation. By this time, they had sold most of their sheep and were running primarily cattle.

J. J. Lopez didn't run the Tejon Ranch from an office, but continuously combed the 350,000 acre ranch, checking on livestock, water, feed, as well as the men working under him. He drove a team of matched sorrel horses hitched to a heavy buckboard. The buckboard was loaded with feed and water for the horses, and food, water and blankets for himself. He also carried a saddle and other

Outstanding Cattlemen honored by the Kern County Branch of the California Cattlemen's Association in 1976. From the left, Louis Rochford, Bob Grisedale, Tony Araujo, Justinian Caire, Leonard Bidart.

Louis Rochford arrived in California in 1932. He became the University of California's first state-wide Extension Livestock Specialist. He developed a state-wide program working closely with the California Cattlemen Association. Rochford became resident manager of the Tejon Ranch in 1943 and eventually moved up in the organization to Chairman of the Board. He retired in 1963. In 1981 he was voted into the Cowboy Hall of Fame in Oklahoma City.

Bob Grisedale was born in Hutton, England, in 1893 and came to the United States when he was fifteen years old. After he completed an eighth grade education he worked for neighboring ranchers in the Weedpatch area. He eventually worked **for the Tehachapi Cattle Company and later had his own ranch in the Granite Station area.**

Antonio (Tony) Araujo born in 1890 in Tehachapi. He was the grandson of Roman Araujo, who arrived in what was later to be Kern County in 1842. Tony cowboyed on the Tejon Ranch for fifty years, the last thirty-five as livestock superintendent. He was directly responsible for 20,000 head of cattle ranging over 350,000 acres of grazing land in the San Joaquin Valley and the Tehachapi Mountains. Tony died in 1982 at the age of ninety-two. Harold Thurber, who made the presentation, described Tony as a "true friend, a fine cattleman and an outstanding cowboy."

Justinian Caire was honored for his years at Santa Clara University and the University of California. In 1952 Caire joined the Kern County Land Company as manager of the California cattle ranch operation. In later years he took over operation of the company's Southern Arizona and New Mexico ranches.

Leonard Bidart became the head of his family at age sixteen upon his father's death. He purchased his first band of ewes in 1923, and in 1941 he bought his first cattle in the Bishop area. Bidart later expanded his ranching operations to the community of McKittrick. He died in 1977.

# Early California Ranches

The discovery of gold in California in 1848 proved to be a boon to the cattle business, as there would soon be thousands of hungry miners to feed. The California Ranchos didn't have this market cornered, because this same year a Texan by the name of T. J. Trimmer drove the first trail herd into California from Texas. He arrived at an opportune time and it was reported that he received one hundred dollars a head for his cattle. Other herds followed him on the trail from Texas the same year. The owners of the herds that left Texas in 1848 hadn't yet heard about the discovery of gold, but were headed for California because of the reports of abundant feed and ideal climate for cattle raising. As fast as they had their cattle fat enough for market, they would drive them to San Francisco and receive top price. The Houston Telegraph, March 8, 1849, reported the following: "Preparing to head for California with a train of emigrants, three or four thousand horses and mules . . . besides numerous herds of cattle."

Cattle continued to come in, and it was reported by California Governor Bigler that just in 1854 alone, 9,000 head of cattle followed the southern route to California.

In 1854, three Texas cattlemen who drove cattle to California left diaries. In 1932, James G. Bell had his story told in a book, *A Log of the Texas to California Cattle Trail 1854,* which was published by Southwest Historical Quarterly, Austin, Texas. Texan John James, owner and driver of another herd, also had his diary published. Of greatest interest to this author was the diary of a former Virginian, Major Michael Erskine, who also trailed cattle from Texas to California in 1854. My interest stemmed from the fact that he settled in the Kern River Valley where he had a gold mine and

mill. As one of the earliest settlers, Erskine Creek was named for him. In 1979, some 125 years after Erskine made his drive, his diary was published by Mary E. Johnston, a fourth generation of the Erskine family, with a historical introduction by Texas historian and cattleman, J. Evetts Haley.

Major Erskine's drive started from his ranch near San Antonio, known then, as it is today, as the

**Michael Erskine in 1854.**
Photo courtesy N.S. Haley Memorial Library, Midland, Texas.

Capote Ranch. It derived its name from a nearby peak called El Capote. Erskine acquired this ranch property in 1843 at public auction from the Republic of Texas for $206.00 in fees and $25.86 in accumulated taxes.

There was a generous stand of timber on the ranch, and from this he cut lumber to build a large home, quarters for his slaves, and a smoke house. (In the 1850 census it stated he owned sixteen slaves). On a part of the ranch he called the Sandies, he built corrals capable of holding 1,000 head of cattle.

By 1849, he had 600 acres of corn and cotton, and in that year harvested 12,000 bushels of corn. He freighted the cotton to Port Lavaca on the coast. In the same year his slaves gathered 600 bushels of pecans from trees that grew wild on his place and these he floated down the Guadalupe River to market.

He was helped with his work on the ranch by his two sons, Michael E. and John, who both later went to California with him, and by another son, Andrew, who stayed at home in Texas on the Capote Ranch. He took them down in canoes chopped from the huge trunks of the native cottonwoods and manned enroute by his Negro slaves.

The census disclosed he was running twenty-eight head of horses and mules, eighteen work oxen, 200 swine, 130 head of milk cows and 300 head of range cattle.

With things going so well for him on his ranch, gold was discovered in California. The senior Erskine suffered, as so many others, from gold fever. A son, Alexander, who was attending school in Virginia, wrote home urging his mother to "use all your endeavors to persuade father from going to California. He is too old to undertake such a wild adventure." He was persuaded for awhile, but in 1854, five years later, at the age of sixty, he decided he was still at the right age.

Erskine purchased 1,054 head of steers and gathered his "outfit," as his paid crew was called. His crew was made up of his two sons, Mike and John, who had acquired a lot of range experience. Also, another kinsman, Ignatious Johnson, his son-in-law, was part of the crew, as well as Henry Maney, who was green at first, but according to Erskine's diary, was a good hand as he gained experience. His paid hands included experienced Mexican hands. He also hired Captain James H. Callahan with a crew of fighting men to follow him. He paid this superb Texas Ranger $1,500 to

make the trip with him. This proved to be a wise decision, as the record shows, especially because of their trouble with the Indians, which was traced with lead, powder and blood. The rest of their crew of thirty-five were working their way to the gold fields. This was quite common. These men received only their food and the protection of the trail outfit while traveling through those many miles of dangerous country.

The remuda of horses made up more than 100 head. Besides these, there were oxen needed to pull the wagons carrying the supplies (chuck wagon?), and an ambulance, or "hack," that Michael Erskine drove with mules to pull it.

The route they would follow from Texas to California started around San Antonio, through El Paso, along the Gila River to the Yuma area, and on into California.

Erskine's diary, as is true of other diaries, showed in print that they felt their day-to-day problems were hardly worth mentioning. These day-to-day problems included many stampedes and steady rain. Sometimes it rained for four days at a time, which turned the trail into a sea of mud and created a lot of extra, and almost impossible, work for the men trying to get the cattle across the swollen rivers.

One part of Erskine's diary that was most interesting to the author took place towards the end of August. They had just left the San Pedro River and turned north towards Santa Cruz, when they picked up and pieced together a letter addressed to Major Erskine. It had been left by the James M. Glenn party. The letter, which had been found and torn up by Indians, told how early in the morning on the 25th of August the Indians had attacked the wagon train and killed young James Houston. They were able to save all 450 head of their cattle; however, twenty head of their horses were run off by the Indians. The cattle in the train belonged to the dead James Houston and his brother-in-law, John Dunlap.

The Glenns and Dunlaps both settled in Linn's Valley where the town of Glennville was later named for James Glenn. One of the young men in the wagon train, Jim Dunlap, later became a pony express rider.

On Monday, the 4th of September, Erskine caught up with the Glenn party, and also the John James, and the Beck and Bryant trail outfits. They were all camped near the little terror-stricken Mexican settlement of Santa Cruz. The Apache In-

James (Jim) Early Dunlap was a Pony Express rider. Uncle Jim, as most people in the Glennville area called him, came to California as a boy with a wagon train in 1854. On the trip the wagon train was attacked by the **Apache Indians and Jim's uncle, James Houston, was** shot and killed. Jim delivered mail (by mule) from Glennville to the Kern River mines in the late 1850's and early 1860's.

dians had been raiding the wagon trains and the small Mexican towns in the area.

Because of all the help they had they decided to try and recover 140 head of cattle belonging to the Beck and Bryant herd which the Indians had driven off, also the twenty head of horses from the Glenn party. They recruited eighteen hands from the trail outfits and twenty Mexican horsemen from the settlement. They left at eight o'clock that night with Captain James Callahan in charge. Callahan went into action in typical Texas Ranger style. They followed the Apaches forty-five miles into Mexico and surprised them in camp.

The initial charge took place on horseback, after which an intense battle continued on foot. The Indians were armed mainly with bows and arrows, while Callahan's men were using shotguns and six-shooters. The Mexicans in his group were using sabers and Mexican lances.

Erskine's son-in-law, Henry Maney, told in later years how one Indian, who was about to get away,

was roped by one of the Mexicans. As the Indian was dragged along the ground another Mexican lanced him to death. They counted twenty-one dead Indians when the battle was over. One account said the scalps of the Indians were taken, "mostly by the Mexicans to get the bounty that was being paid by the Mexican government." A fifteen year old Mexican boy who had been taken captive by the Indians was recovered and later returned to his family in Tucson. They recovered sixty-five head of cattle, ten head of horses and a team of mules. An arrow was pulled from the arm of the only trail hand to be wounded, and the body of a Mexican who had been killed was taken back to his family in Santa Cruz.

After a very eventful trip, they finally arrived in California on the 10th of November, 1854. It had taken them six months and six days to make what I believe was one of the longest and hardest of any of the cattle drives made across the face of America, but not once did Erskine express despair or concern in his diary. They stopped the herd on an unclaimed range near what was known as the Warner Ranch. They made their camp, and after fixing up some old corrals, they branded the 814 head that had survived the trip.

His crew was now a well-organized outfit pointed out by the fact that they branded the whole herd in two days. They had to rope each animal (most of them big steers) by the head and heels and

James Madison Glenn, founder of the town of Glennville. Although Glenn didn't bring any cattle with him, he was the captain of the wagon train with which the Dunlaps were traveling.

stretch them out on the ground before branding them. They decided to winter the cattle here and in the spring drive the herd the remaining 600 miles to San Francisco, which at that time was the only available market. They also had to try to get them in shape to sell, as the trip had left them in poor condition.

Erskine then paid off the bulk of his crew, who were anxious to take off to the gold fields, and on November 18th, after leaving the herd in the charge of his son, John, he pulled out for Los Angeles.

It took him, plus five men, five days to make the 113 miles, which wasn't bad with the trail-worn horses they were driving. Upon arriving in Los Angeles, he loaded the wagons with provisions for the winter and started his son, Mike, and one of his Texas trail hands, Joe Shelley, back to the herd.

Two days later, he, Maney, Callahan, and Box Roberts left San Pedro by steamer for San Francisco. He stayed there while the others caught a ship for the long journey back to Texas via the Horn.

By spring of 1855, Erskine had located a range for his cattle about seven miles out of Stockton, and had his sons, John and Mike, start trailing them north at about ten miles a day. During this time, he put up 125 tons of hay on the land he had rented. In 1856, he still had 700 head of cattle one hundred miles north of San Francisco and was still trying to get them sold. Even the ones he did sell he had trouble collecting the money for. In November of 1856, Erskine left for the gold fields of the Kern River and left his sons to continue trying to sell the herd. In 1857, his sons sold the balance of the cattle to Miller and Lux and joined their father on the Kern River.

On the Kern River, he purchased a mine south of the hot springs, about where the town of Bodfish is located today, and put all his energy in it to try and recoup the losses he was realizing on his cattle. He had put what cash he had received from cattle sales into the mine and mill, besides signing notes on the balance.

The irony of the situation was that Erskine's lode was obviously rich, running from $20.00 to $300.00 per ton in gold. However, due to lack of technology, they were not able to save much of the gold. He then borrowed more money and sent a friend, Mr. Chevalier, to purchase expensive machinery to try and save the gold.

The editor of the *Visalia Delta,* in his report on gold mining on the Kern River, wrote, "Mr.

Erskine and sons on the opposite side of the river are running two stampers. This mill is run by water power, supplied by a spring. These gentlemen have expended much time and money adding complicated machinery to their mill, all of which proved a failure, and they have returned to the original stampers with galvanized plates below the battery."

From the fall of 1854, there had been a flow of correspondence between Michael Erskine and his family in Texas. Many of the letters are included in the book with his diary. Although conditions in California were extremely unprofitable, according to his letters, he was the most optimistic man that ever lived.

To make matters worse, things had gone badly back in Texas. In 1856 and '57, one of the most devastating droughts in history hit the region around Erskine's ranch, drying up range and crops as well. Everything in Texas was mortgaged to the hilt, and before he got back to Texas, everything had to be sold, with the exception of some of his range cattle. The only letter that expressed discouragement was one where he asked that his favorite old donkey not be sold.

At his mine on the Kern River, his son, John, came down with rheumatism and his other son, Mike, crushed his hand in their stamp mill, leaving both of them crippled for life. The two boys stuck by their father right to the last days of his California venture and stayed in the Hot Springs Valley (Lake Isabella) trying to get the gold mine to pay. When their father returned to Texas about the first of July, 1859, he went back hoping to find some way to pay his debts. Interest was running three to four percent and the total continued to mount. He had been gone five years since he had so proudly headed his herd of longhorns into the sun from his pens on what they called the Sandies. Like so many others who left everything to go to California, Erskine had gambled unwisely and lost.

When Michael Erskine arrived back in Texas, there was still cattle running loose on the range, and gathering the best he could find bearing his brand, he headed another small herd for market in the fall of 1861. This time, he chose New Orleans, which had offered a market since the days of the Spanish ranches in Texas.

In April of 1862, he wrote back to his family from New Orleans that his first lot of eighty head had sold well, although "poor beef." He figured that they would average thirty dollars each, which would pay a profit after all expenses. He closed out the sales of his cattle and started back to Texas. He got only as far as New Iberia, Louisiana, where on May 5, 1862, his heart played out on him and he died. He had made one last gamble on a cattle drive and again he had lost.

While the first large herds came into California by the southern route, greater numbers came in over the northern route, often called the California Trail. In 1849, a fort was established on this trail along the North Platte River in Nebraska. Known as Fort Kearney, it was garrisoned by a few companies of regulars. The commanding officer ordered the guard to count the wagons and estimate the number of livestock that passed the Fort that year. In 1850, Walter Crow and his four sons drove five hundred head of Durham cattle to California. Because his drive was one of the first over this trail, it served as a model for later drives. Crow and his sons established a ranch on Orestimba Creek, and it was for him and his family that the old town of Crows Landing is named.

The largest jump in livestock traveling over this trail occurred in 1852. In that year, it was estimated that over 100,000 head of livestock passed on their way to California. My grandfather, John W. Powers, had been to the gold fields in 1849. He returned to Missouri, and in 1852, he brought his new bride and a "large drove of cattle" via the northern route into California.

Dolly Evaline Powers came over Donner Pass with her husband in 1852.

The year 1853 brought another big increase; 5,577 horses, 2,190 mules, 105,792 cattle, and 48,495 sheep were counted. In this year, 15,219 people were on the trail with 3,708 wagons.

Of more importance to the livestock business than the numbers coming, was the fact that this year the first purebred cattle were among those traveling to California. This was a herd of one hundred Durham cattle, part of which were registered, owned by John Alexander McCray. McCray, a native of Nova Scotia, was traveling west with his wife, a former Pennsylvania Dutch girl, Margaret Learn, and three children. Starting in Indiana, they were traveling with the trail herd of 900 head of longhorns belonging to a Welchman by the name of Johnny Roberts. The McCray children called him Uncle Johnny, but I don't know how he was related. Little is known about the trip west except that on August 5, 1853 at Donner Lake, a second son was born to Margaret McCray. Named John, he, along with his father's red and blue roan Durham cattle, made a big impact on the cattle business of central California.

Nothing more is known about the Roberts cattle, but the McCrays settled first at Crows Landing in Tuolumne County. (In 1850, California had become the thirty-first state, with nineteen counties being formed.) After staying in Tuolumne County three years, they moved south to Squaw Valley, east of Fresno. The McCrays stayed there three years, being forced to move because the grizzly bears were eating the calves from the Durham herd as fast as they were born.

Their next move was near what would later become the site of Bakersfield. This was in December of 1859. They settled near the Kern River, close to what is now the foot of the China Grade. The McCrays moved into an old adobe house with a thatched roof made of native tules. Near their home, and above the China Grade crossing of the Kern River, was a shallow hole dug in the river bank. People came here to get oil to grease their wagons and machinery. Alexander McCray had the oil analyzed, but was told it had no commercial value. At this time, nobody dreamed of the possibilities of this "black gold." It wasn't until forty years later, in 1899, that the Kern River oil field was developed.

While living on the Kern River, McCray became acquainted with David Alexander. They were both Scotsmen and the main cattlemen in the area at this time. They became fast friends and Alexander bought all of McCray's bull calves from his herd of Durham cattle.

They remained at this location a few years, but because of all the swamp land nearby, many of the family came down with malaria. The McCrays moved north to Poso Creek, not far from the Butterfield stage station. The Butterfield stage line had been established in 1858, and the route skirted the San Joaquin Valley on the east side as there were too many sloughs to cross in the center of the valley. Coming south from the station at Visalia, it went twenty-five miles to Tule River (later named Porterville in 1864). Continuing along through the foothills for fifteen miles, it came to the Fountain Springs station, and then another twelve miles to Mountain House. Fifteen miles farther on was Poso Creek, then nine miles to Gordon's Ferry where it crossed the Kern River. After proceeding twelve miles to Kern River Slough, it continued another fourteen miles to the sink of Tejon, thirteen miles to Fort Tejon and over the Tejon Pass, on past Reed's place in Los Angeles County.

While the McCray family were living at Poso Creek in 1860, the first settler moved to the Kern River Slough, later called Bakersfield. This was a man by the name of Christian Bohna. He built a house of cottonwood logs and thatched it with tules. He cleared ten acres and planted corn, harvesting 110 bushels per acre. In 1861, Dr. Sparrell Woody joined him, and Bohna's daughter, Sarah Louise, married Dr. Woody. The 1862 flood came along, flooding out the Bohnas and Woodys. Christian Bohna moved to Oregon, not returning to Kern County until 1870. Dr. Woody moved to higher ground at the foot of Blue Mountain, northeast of Bakersfield. Here Dr. Woody established a ranch, and he and his family became leading cattle ranchers in the area. In 1889, a settlement that sprang up three miles from his ranch was named for Dr. Woody.

Many other pioneer cattle ranches were being established in the mountain sections surrounding the San Joaquin Valley in the 1860's, of which quite a few are run by the descendants today. Near Granite Station were the ranches of James F. Williams and Robert L. Stockton, each of whom married a daughter of David Engle, who had a stock ranch in the same area. Near Glennville were David Lavers and John Dunlap. Samuel Sneaden started a cattle ranch near Frazier Mountain. During these years, Grant P. Cuddeback was running cattle around Tehachapi and on the Mojave Desert to the east. Fred Fickert also ran his cattle around Tehachapi.

Henry Bohna, a rancher from the Woody area.

George Cummings ranged his cattle in the valley named for him, and in the same general area, John Moore Brite and his family had a good-sized cattle operation in Brites Valley.

William Carol (Billie) Boen, early-day Kern County cattleman. His home ranch is still used by his grandchildren, great-grandchildren, and great-great-grandchildren.

Tobias Meadow cow camp in 1900. In front from the left, Jeff Carver, Natch (John) Carver. Natch was killed at this camp a short time later when his mule bucked into the end of one of the cabins.

Carver Bowen in 1976, a Glennville cattleman.

Taken at the Wire Corrals on Breckenridge Road (about 25 miles east of Bakersfield) after branding O'Rielly calves. Bill Sheppard ran the outfit. From the left in back, Darrel Degler, Ernest Seeley, Jim Dean, Fred Harmon, Cliff Record, Remick Albitre, Glen Record. In front from the left, Slim Evans, Hugh Smith, Bill Sheppard, Ken Mebane, William Petersen, Louie Mebane, Dan Garcia.

The Record family in 1958. From left: sons Wes, Clint, Glen, and Rex, and their father Cliff.

Carl Carver (left) with Ward Woody in 1980.

**Granite Station Cattlemen in 1964. Hugh Smith (left) and Bob Grisedale.**

From left: Frank Smoot, H. Guy Hughes and Jim Polkinghorn at the Burke Ranch on the Little Poso, in 1909.

Louie Monotti in 1955 at age 70 with his horse "Dick," age 37.

Gerald Carver, grandson of Joel and Louisa Carver.

Henry Bowen, a Glennville cattleman.

O.H. (Walt) Klein. One of the first rangers at Isabella. He later started a cattle ranch in the White River-Glennville area.

Hiram G. (Guy) Hughes in 1970 on his favorite horse, Dusty. Guy's grandfather, Hiram Hughes, was the captain of a wagon train that came across the plains in 1850. Guy's father, William B. Hughes was born in Missouri and was only nine months old when he was brought to California by his parents. Guy was born on the Hughes' homestead near Glennville in 1887.

Bruno Contreras, an old time cowboy from the Glennville area who cowboyed on Greenhorn Mountain. Bruno lived to the age of 100.

Thea Nash, pioneer school teacher and ranch owner in the Glennville area.

Jesse W. Smith, Sr.

Jesse W. Smith, Jr., cowboy and horse breaker.

Hadley Frazier, a Glennville rancher, and his hunting dog, Old Spot. Hunting was, and still is, a favorite hobby of most cowboys.

Lawrence Snow, a Walker Basin cattleman.

Louie Mebane and his grandson, Chet.

From the left, Jim Ben Williams, Kenneth Mebane and John Rofer at Rofer's calf branding in 1976.

Aubrey Pascoe, an early forest ranger and cowboy.

After mining near Havilah in the 1860's, Angus M. Crites moved three miles north of Havilah and established a ranch on Clear Creek. This ranch was later owned by Walker Rankin and Jim Polkinghorn. In Walker Basin, both Walker Rankin, Sr., and his brother-in-law, A. T. Lightner, Sr., had cattle ranches, as did Nick Williams, William Weldon, and Daniel Waggoner Walser.

On the South Fork of the Kern River were the ranches of Thomas H. Smith and John Nicoll, Sr., as well as the pioneer ranches of Grant, Mack, Barrows, and J. V. Roberts.

The Tejon Rancho was still going strong during this period. However, by the early 1880's, it became apparent to General Beale that this ranch was better suited for cattle than for sheep, and a gradual change was made until the Tejon Rancho ran mostly cattle. Before General Beale's death in 1889, his ranch covered a total of 270,000 acres. In 1912, General Beale's son, Truxtun Beale, and Beale's widow sold the ranch to a prominent group of Los Angeles businessmen consisting of Harry Chandler, Moses Sherman and twenty-eight of their friends and associates. In 1936, this group converted the ranch into a publicly-owned company; it continued into the 1980's as one of Kern County's most modern ranches.

By 1863, the bears on Poso Creek started eating

McCray's Durham calves. To escape the bears, and also to put his children near a school, he moved to Visalia, where a school had first opened on the 17th of September 1855. Here, Mr. McCray homesteaded 160 acres of land. He went into the mountains and whip-sawed lumber by hand to build a home.

When the McCray family moved to Visalia, they became acquainted with Aquilla and Walker Rankin. The Rankin brothers had been in the dairy business in Contra Costa County. In 1859, they moved to Mill Creek near Visalia where they went into the cattle business. The Rankins and McCrays had both originally come from Indiana County, Pennsylvania, and although they had at one time lived only forty miles from each other, it seems they had not met until they were in Visalia. Sometime during 1866, John Alexander McCray sold Walker Rankin quite a few of his Shorthorn cattle. Walker Rankin took them to Walker Basin when he moved his cattle operation there during 1867. His Shorthorn cattle not only greatly improved the native longhorns that were there when he arrived, but also spread to nearby areas such as the Kern River Valley.

The elder McCray had no more than finished his home when he became ill with pneumonia and died. With the death of John Alexander McCray, John and his older brother, Charlie, were left with the responsibility of taking care of their mother, two sisters, and a younger brother, so they quit school and went to work. At the time, John was only thirteen years old and Charlie was fifteen, but you grew up fast in those days.

The two McCray boys went to work for the Merhten brothers. This German family raised not only cattle, but a large number of horses. The Merhten brothers furnished hundreds of horses for the Butterfield Stage, and John and his brother helped break and deliver them. At that time, the Telegraph Stage Company line branched off at Fountain Springs, going through Glennville, over Greehorn Mountain to Kernville, then, after a stop at Scodie's store at Onyx and a stop at the Thomas Smith stage station at Canebrake, it proceeded over Walker Pass to Coyote Holes (also called Freeman's Station). At this station, which was located two miles west of the present Freeman Junction, it intersected the Los Angeles-Lone Pine Stage and returned to Visalia.

By 1868, the range around Visalia was getting crowded, so the two McCray boys took their Dur-

**Walker Rankin, Sr.**

ham herd back to the Kern River Slough. Many changes had taken place in the last five years. Most of the changes were brought about by Colonel Thomas Baker, the founder of Bakersfield. In 1863, Colonel Baker moved his family into the adobe house built by Christian Bohna. Baker had been elected State Senator from Tulare and Fresno Counties. He served for the 1861 and '62 sessions, then in 1862, in partnership with Harvey S. Brown, he purchased the swamp franchise owned by Montgomery, Downes, and Samson. With the help of thirty Indians from the Sebastian Reservation, he set to work reclaiming 400,000 acres of swamp and overflow land. He finally acquired a total of 87,120 acres under the terms of the Swamp and Overflow Act of 1851. When Kern County was formed in 1866, he began to survey the proposed city of Bakersfield. He fenced off a field and planted alfalfa just east of the present site of the civic center on Truxtun Avenue. The boundaries of his field were between 14th and 17th street, and "K" and "P" Streets.

Travelers who were enroute from Los Angeles to San Francisco were advised to stop at "Baker's field" where they could graze their animals. Baker is reported to have said to the travelers, "Help yourself, but don't waste anything."

By 1868, when the McCrays moved back to the

Colonel Thomas A. Baker, the founder of the town of Bakersfield.

Bakersfield area, there was a post office in George B. Chester's store on the corner of 19th and Chester. By 1870, Coswell and Ellis also had a store, and the Kern County Courier was being published. There was a blacksmith and carriage shop owned by Fred Mackin and a harness shop owned by Phillip Reinstein. Littlefield and Philan had opened a livery stable and John B. Tungate had opened his saloon. There was also a school with fifty students, and two rooming houses.

In the late 1860's, Wellington Canfield and Ferdinand A. Tracy were running cattle in the area of the Kern River Slough. They operated from several cattle camps located on Buena Vista Slough, but later operated from the Canfield Ranch six miles southwest of Bakersfield.

In 1868, Miller and Lux started running cattle around Kern River and Buena Vista Slough. In about the same year, James C. Crocker started acquiring land and cattle for Miller and Lux and he operated the Crocker Ranch in the Temblor Range about six miles out of Bakersfield. The Miller and Lux ranch had been purchasing land and cattle at a steady rate for the previous ten years and were destined to be the largest land owners in the United States. Henry Miller was the driving force behind the partnership. It all started when Miller, a German immigrant, arrived in San Francisco in 1850 with six dollars in his pocket. Henry had run away from home at fifteen. Before he left, he had been trained by his father in the art of raising and slaughtering livestock, as well as marketing them. When Henry was eight years old and out herding the family calves, he had seen a herd of cattle with the letter "H" branded on their left hip. That night, he dreamed of a vast range in America covered with his cattle all branded, not with an "H," but with a double "H," and the vision never left him. From that day on he vowed to go to America and own a big cattle ranch.

After coming to America, he worked for someone else for only one year. In 1851, after the big fire in San Francisco, he took possession of a lot on Jackson Street and opened a butcher shop of his own. He slaughtered calves and carried them on his back to North Beach and other parts of the city. Generally, the beef brought to San Francisco during the gold rush days was of inferior quality, but Miller's secret was to go to bed early and be at the stock yards at the first light to have the pick of the stock.

As cattle became more scarce around San Francisco, cattle were being brought in from greater distances. Henry Miller began hearing fragmented information about a great cattle country to the south known as the San Joaquin Valley. When he was sorting some hides, his eye was quick to see a particularly large one with a fine reddish color. Turning it over, he examined it to see if any cuts had been made in this fine specimen. As he turned it to where the left hip came into view, he saw through the skin the clear outline of the brand. He received a real shock because it was the HH, double H brand he had dreamt about as a boy. He finally remembered he had received a bunch of cattle from a man by the name of Hildreth from the San Joaquin Valley. Before long, he was planning a long trip; one to the land of his dreams.

To make a long story short, he found the ranch he sought. It was one quarter of a Spanish grant along the west side of the San Joaquin River known as Rancho Sanjon de Santa Rita, named after the patron saint of women about to become mothers. The ranch was covered with luxurious grass and abundant water. Cattle with the HH brand grazed along the river, and he knew he had to have this place. He met a cattleman who was booted and spurred and riding a fine horse. Everything else was poverty-stricken and forlorn, as the owner, Hildreth, had no love for the cattle business and wanted to be off to the mines. In the course of their conversation, Hildreth stated that he would like to sell the place. Before Miller mounted his horse to return to San Francisco, he had an option in his pocket to buy 8,835 acres of the Ranch Sanjon de Santa Rita for one dollar and fifteen cents per acre, and also 7,500 head of cattle at five dollars a head. Included was the Double "H" brand.

On his way north, he visited all the ranches and became acquainted with the cattlemen of the region. Usually before he left, he had an option in his pocket for their fat cattle.

Upon his return to San Francisco, he went to William C. Rolston, his banker, to show him the contract with Hildreth and the other options. He gave a glowing account of the country and had a few figures to show how he could bring in a profit on the cattle. The banker was impressed and agreed that the bank would advance the money. The year was 1858 when he went into partnership with Charles Lux under the name of Miller and Lux, with the understanding that he would take care of the cattle and land and Lux would take care of the business in the city. They started on a spree of buying land and cattle that didn't end until thirty years later. Miller's dusty figure on horseback soon became a familiar sight throughout California. Night or day, rain or shine, he could be seen driving cattle on their long journey to market, employing vaqueros, buying hay, getting water, or moving supplies. One of Miller's favorite sayings was, "I only consider sleeping a necessity, and many times I have wished I could do without eating." He would get up at five in the morning and work until eleven at night if necessary. At each of his more than 100 ranches, a room was kept in readiness for him.

Miller, like so many ranch owners in the west, took advantage of the excellent Spanish, Mexican and Indian vaqueros and made many of them his superintendents on his many ranches. Two of these were Narcisco Jesus Castro, majordomo on his Bloomfield Ranch, and Antone Lopez, majordomo for Miller's cattle operation in the Los Banos area. These men and their crews drove cattle Miller had purchased from ranches such as the Tejon Ranch to Butchertown in south San Francisco.

When his partner, Charles Lux, died in 1887, he bought his share from the heirs in Germany, allowing him sole control. This story could go on and on, but I will end it by saying that by the time of his death in 1916, he owned more land than any other person in the United States. His empire covered 14,000,000 acres in California, Nevada and Oregon. At one time, he owned over a million head of livestock, banks, hotels, stores, public utilities, and slaughter houses; in fact, just about all the en-

John Peyron, a French/Indian who worked for the Miller and Lux Ranch. He is pictured with his younger brother, Albert.

terprises and property in three San Joaquin towns. At one time, a man could ride horseback from the Mexican border to Oregon and stay on Miller property every night.

Some twelve years after Miller's death, a friend and neighbor of mine, Clifford Cross, worked for several years on three of the ranches in the San Joaquin Valley. They still called it the Miller and Lux outfit and it still used the double H brand. The main difference was that instead of driving cattle the length of California, they moved them by railroad, bringing cattle south from Oregon and from Nevada and Arizona to graze on the pasture in the San Joaquin Valley. In the summer many were fattened in feed lots and the mother-stock shipped by rail back to their home range. However, the ranches were steadily going downhill as there was no one around that would take care of the thousand of small details like the immigrant from Wuerttemberg, Germany.

In 1874, a new land and cattle company came into the San Joaquin Valley that was to give Miller and Lux its most bitter competition. The business partnership of this company started in 1849 when James Haggin and Lloyd Tevis, both young Kentuckians, met in the gold fields of California. They married sisters and made their money selling mining claims and land in general. They also lent money quite profitably, sometimes at interest as high as fifteen percent.

The first land they accumulated in Kern County was in partnership with W. B. Carr. Carr had been a political Napolean for the Southern Pacific Railroad, and he was a driving force in the acquisition of land and water. The first large block of land purchased was the 87,120 acres Baker had reclaimed near the town of Bakersfield. This block of land they purchased from Livermore and Redington. The next purchase was 52,000 acres lying southwest of Bakersfield, known as the Gates Tract. These acres were purchased cheaply because of the threat of malaria around the lakes. About the same time, Haggin, Tevis, and Carr established the Bellevu and McClung ranches. The company was incorporated in 1890 as the Kern County Land Company and buying of land and acquisition of water rights to irrigate these acres finally made the company the "greatest irrigated farm in the world," with a total of 400,000 acres. During the 1870's and '80's, the Kern County Land's biggest competitor was the Miller and Lux Cattle Company. This was especially true when it came to water to irrigate the vast acreage each of these companies owned. It was taken to the courts in 1881 and continued until 1888. It ended with the Kern County Land Company getting seventy-five percent of the water from the Kern River.

The success of the Kern County Land Company all during its existence was due, in a great part, to its choice of men. One of these men was Frank G. Drum, who joined the organization in 1887. Listed as the Vice President, he was a real financial genius who ran the operation from the ranch office in San Francisco. Another employee who helped the Kern County Land Company was Henry Jastro. Jastro went to work for this company in 1874 and worked his way up until he was chosen manager in 1903, a job he held until 1924. Billy Carr died in 1897, Tevis died in 1899, and Drum died in 1925.

In 1904, John McCray went to work for the Kern County Land Company as manager of the cattle operation, a job which he held until his death in 1924. His son, Clint, took the job and held it until 1957. In 1947, there were 100,000 head of cattle being run by the Kern County Land Company in New Mexico, California, and Oregon.

Another large cattleman in the 1860's and '70's was a Frenchman by the name of Chenac, who had a homestead in the lower end of Cummings Valley. In 1896, this ranch was sold to Ross G. Hill, passed

to his son, Roland G. Hill, and finally became owned by the Tehachapi Cattle Company.

This book, thus far, has dealt mostly with cattle and very little has been said about the sheep in California. For the first 110 years of livestock in California (1769-1879), sheep far outnumbered cattle. It has been estimated that by 1825, the sheep that Father Junipero Serra had brought in to establish the string of missions in California had increased to one million head, and besides this, private individuals owned another million. There was a series of droughts in California from 1828 to 1830 and sheep died by the thousands. After these droughts, just as the flocks were building up again, in 1840-41 there was another dry year and a large number died. Because of this, there weren't large numbers of sheep available when gold was discovered in 1848. The miners preferred beef to mutton. However, at this time, individuals started bringing large numbers of sheep in from other states such as

Clint and Marie McCray. Clint took over the management of the Kern County Land Company cattle operation in the San Joaquin Valley in 1924. He held this position until 1957. In 1947 McCray sent the author to ride with the ZX wagon in Oregon.

New Mexico, and many of the early miners were fed more mutton than beef.

Early in the 19th century, Don Bartolomé Baca, who at that time was Governor of Spanish New Mexico, had two million sheep on his 1,282,000 acre grant outside Albuquerque. His herds were tended by 2,700 herders, who stayed out with the sheep all year. There were so many sheep in New Mexico, they were worth less than a dollar a head.

When the news of the gold rush reached New Mexico, some of the ranchers were quick to take advantage of it. In 1847, Miguel Otera and Antonio Jose Luna drove 25,000 sheep from Santa Fe to southern California. From there they headed up through the San Joaquin Valley to Sacramento where they sold them to the hungry miners for prices ranging from ten to twenty-five dollars per head.

Some of the Americans also started taking advantage of this. In 1853, Kit Carson, the famed mountain man and Indian scout, bought 6,500 head of sheep. Even though he paid two dollars and fifty cents per head, after he made his drive from Santa Fe to Sacramento, he made $30,000 profit. As he was on his way back to New Mexico, where he bought a ranch with his profits, he reported seeing 100,000 head of sheep on their way to California. It is a conservative estimate that at least 500,000 sheep were trailed from New Mexico to California between 1850 and 1860.

These sheep from New Mexico were descendants of the little churro sheep brought over from Spain to start the missions. While they were good to eat, they did not produce a good wool crop. Many coming west during the gold rush brought sheep to feed the miners, hoping to make a good profit. In 1853 alone, 48,495 head of sheep were counted by the army as they passed Fort Kearney, Nebraska. Of course, many of these were used to feed the miners; still, sheep definitely outnumbered the cattle in California. Even in the San Joaquin Valley in the 1850's and '60's, sheep outnumbered cattle.

The sheep business flourished in California in the 1860's. Prize imports were being brought in to improve the original churro strain. Of these new breeds, the one to do the most for the sheep industry in the Kern County area was French Merino. In 1860, Soloman Jewett drove a band of these fine-wooled imported Merino sheep all the way from Vermont, bringing them to what would later be Kern County. Jewett ran his sheep with Colonel Vineyard on the Tejon Ranch.

Between 1860 and 1870, there were a growing number of sheepmen who used Kern County as their headquarters. General Beale of the El Tejon Ranch ran 100,000 head and Miller and Lux at one time ran 200,000 head. In his book, *The Golden Empire Kern County, California,* Eugene Burmeister lists other sheepmen of that period. They included, "Simon Wible, who had a ranch west of Bakersfield, Harry Quinn, who ran sheep east of Delano, Peter Lambert of Granite Station, Pierre Sartial of San Emigdio, Antonne Pauly and John D. Chinette of Tehachapi and Faustino Noriega." The Kern County Land Company, which was formed in 1874, also ran about 70,000 head of sheep.

Besides the local sheep owners, French and Basque sheepmen also brought herds through the San Joaquin Valley from the coast, and as the local cattlemen said, "Drove them fast enough to strip the ground bare."

Sheep raising started to decline faster than cattle raising, mostly because of the decline of wool prices in 1873. Also, because so many sheepmen owned very little property and ran their sheep year round on open range, which was beginning to be bought and fenced by many of the big cattlemen, such as Miller and Lux, Kern County Land Company, and the Tejon Ranch, limiting feed. A drought in 1877 also added to their problems.

In the 1860's and much of the 1870's, cattle grazed without any restrictions from the Kings River all the way south to the sinks of the Tejon. To the east of the San Joaquin Valley, they could roam freely to Tehachapi Valley and on east to the Mojave Desert. In 1851, the State Legislature passed a law stating the cattlemen had to hold rodeos. This is what is called a roundup today.

Because of all the herds running together, there would be many problems that would come up. The main problem was, which cattlemen had the right to put his brand on an animal which had left its mother before being branded. These unbranded animals were sometimes called Orejano (O-ray-han'-no). It was because of this problem and others that might come up that it was decided a judge would be appointed for each rodeo.

At least twice a year, and sometimes three times, the country would be worked. The area worked would cover most of what is now Kings, Tulare and Kern counties, with the exception of the Mojave Desert. There would be from 100 to 200 cowboys working together. John McCray, who, with his brothers, were grazing their cattle around the Kern

River Slough, told later that sometimes there would be as many as three hundred cowboys working together, and that a whiskey wagon traveled with the crew. Can't you just imagine two hundred cowboys turned loose in camp each night with a whiskey wagon to draw refreshments from? Four or five hundred head of cattle would be worked each day. The pay was only $15.00 to $20.00 per month, but it was the most sought after work in the San Joaquin Valley.

The main rodeo was the one in June. Branding the calves that had been born since last spring made up a big part of each rodeo. Each owner or a representative of the owner would go into the herd and cut out each cow and calf belonging to his brand. Then, as they were held away from the main herd, the calves would be roped and dragged from the herd to be branded, earmarked, and the bull calves castrated. While one owner was branding his calves, another owner or representative of an owner would be cutting out his cows with unbranded calves on the other side of the herd. There were quite a few calves that had not been branded the year before, and at this time, would not be following their mothers, and this was where the judge of the rodeo came into play. The judge would have to make a determination as to whose brand would be put on the animal.

This job of cutting the herd and branding was the spice of life to these cowboys. Everybody pitched in, making it seem more like play than work. If the cattle which were rounded up were off their home range, the owners would move them back. If they were to be driven any distance, the calves wouldn't be branded until the drive was finished. After locating them on their summer range in the higher mountains, they would brand the calves and turn them loose. Before turning the stock cattle loose, all the big three- and four-year-old steers would be cut out. When all the market steers had been gathered, they were started for Butcher Town in south San Francisco. They would drive the steers only about six miles a day, letting them feed on the way. It would take about two months to make the trip. This way, they would arrive at the market with a few added pounds.

In 1874, the State Legislature passed a law making the stockmen responsible for keeping their cattle and sheep off planted acreage. This, more than anything else, brought to an end the days when herds of livestock roamed at will with little care or supervision. By this time, the amount of grazing and available water for stock was diminishing, because water was being diverted from the natural sloughs and lakes to irrigate large acreage belonging to the Kern County Land Company and other land holders. Drought, too, had taken its toll, such as the one in 1863-64. The face of the vast pastureland, one time spotted with cattle, sheep, herds of antelope, and elk, was taking on a new look. With the shortage of feed, it was no more the Garden of Eden for stock producers.

# The Landers Cattle Company (Onyx Ranch)

Returning to the McCray family . . . where Charlie McCray went after running the family cattle near Bakersfield, we do not know; and after the mother, Margaret, remarried, we lose track of her two young daughters, Sarah and Marilla; also, her small son, Alexander. We do know that by 1871, when young John McCray was eighteen, he was working for two cattlemen by the name of Mence and Murray. They ran their cattle from where Lemon Cove is now to what was known as Buena Vista Lake, and had their headquarters in Porter-

John McCray, a pioneer cattleman of Kern County. After working for Bill Landers for thirty years, John took over the cattle operation for the Kern County Land Company. He managed the operation from 1906 until his death in 1924.

ville. It wasn't long before John was made foreman. John had gone to school only a short time, but always read a lot, devouring books on history, geography, and biographies. As a young man, he learned to speak and write Spanish fluently and could speak the local Indian tongue, as well. When taking part in local spelling bees, he almost always won. He was very good at figuring in his head, and by guessing weight, could figure the selling price of a large herd of cattle.

While foreman of Mence and Murray, John rode into the mining town of Kernville with some of his crew who were looking for fun. He was a six-foot-two redheaded cowboy and as bashful as they come. On this trip, he was spied by pretty and vivacious Ellen Cummings. Ellen was sixteen at the time, and with her black hair and black eyes, love for fun and gaiety, was easily the belle of the town. When she saw the handsome red-headed cowboy, she immediately decided that he was her man. One year later, on November 5th, 1877, they were married. Ellen was the daughter of a family who had crossed the plains in covered wagons from Missouri. She was born on August 11, 1861 at White River where her family ran a hotel. Soon after her birth, they moved to Kernville, where her mother started another hotel on the south edge of Kernville.

Running cattle on the same range as Mence and Murray was a Texas cattleman by the name of William Landers. In 1877, there was a bad drought, and as there wasn't enough feed for all the cattle on that one range, Mr. Landers decided to move his operation to the South Fork of the Kern River. Mr. Landers was impressed with John McCray's ability to handle cattle and offered him a foreman job at $60.00 per month. As this was quite a bit more than he was making, he took the job. Before leaving

Ellen McCray with her mother, May Cummings. May (Mother) Cummings weighed over 300 pounds, and had a heart as big as her body. There is a legend as to how the town Tailholt, where May settled, got its name. When she and her husband came into town, Mother Cummings was hanging onto the tail of her milk cow to get a pull up the last steep stretch. When kidded about it, she replied, "A tail holt is better than no holt at all." Thus the name Tailholt. She ran a hotel in Tailholt for many years. In 1870, after her husband died, she moved her family to Kernville and started a hotel there. She was buried in the old Kernville cemetery.

riding with the crew much of the time. Her closest neighbors lived six miles away, and although some Indian women came to visit Mrs. McCray, they would just sit out in the yard and work on the beautiful baskets they made. Because they spoke hardly any English, very little conversation took place. Andy Brown had a store at Weldon and William Scodie also had one at Onyx; both had post offices. These stores were each about twenty miles one way from the McCray cow camp. Kernville, the closest town of any size, was about forty miles away and entailed a one-day trip each way with horse and buggy.

Their daughter, May, told about when she was five years old, the excitement she felt when she would hear the cattle, as a herd, being brought in; about her mother fixing a big supper for the cowboys; and going down with her father early the next morning to eat breakfast with her father and the crew at the chuck wagon.

In 1885, Mr. Landers built a house for John McCray on the Mack Ranch at Weldon and the family moved in. May started attending the Weldon School, which was just one-half mile away. The same year, an eleven pound boy named John Leland was born into the McCray family. Called Johnnie by the family, he died with spinal meningitis when he was eight years old. In 1889, Clinton Calvin was born. Clint, as he was called, was cowboying for Mr. Landers by the time he was thirteen years old, riding beside his father on the desert range. This old house on the Mack Ranch was still

Mence and Murray, he recommended a young Mexican by the name of Jose Perez to take his place as foreman, and the company gave Jose the job.

Not too long after getting married, John McCray quit Mr. Landers and opened a butcher shop in Kernville. He had plenty of business, but it turned out that many of his good customers bought on credit and failed to pay their bills. Because of this, his business didn't pay very well.

On August 26, 1878, while John and Ellen were living in Kernville, a daughter was born. They named her May. After two years in the butcher business, John went broke, so he went back to work for Mr. Landers. On the Landers range in Kelso Valley, there was a small line shack and a fenced meadow for the horses. It was to this little line shack that John McCray moved his wife and little two-year old daughter. John built a little bedroom for the baby on the south side of the house. It was a lonely life for Ellen McCray, as John was out

The line shack where Tip Tipton, Sr. lives in Kelso Valley. This building was built on the same spot as the one which Landers built for John McCray around 1877. The original was destroyed by fire c. 1900.

standing some 102 years later, but wasn't being used as a dwelling. Mr. Landers sent back to Georgia and had fruit trees sent out by rail for the McCrays. It wasn't long before they had a fine orchard, and also a large garden. Mr. Landers had sent back east for trees five years earlier and planted them on the home ranch. He had planted peaches, pears, and other varieties. These trees produced the best fruit in the area. Everyone in the South Fork Valley was free to come and pick what they needed for their own use at no charge.

On the South Fork, as in many pioneer communities, everyone helped their neighbors whenever needed with no question of getting reimbursed. Ellen McCray was no exception and was always ready to help her neighbors in time of sickness or childbirth. Many times when there was no transportation, she would walk as far as two miles to help take care of a mother and infant and cook for the rest of the family.

For many years, the closest doctor was in Bakersfield, and midwives such as Sophie Smith delivered most of the babies in the South Fork Valley. A

May McCray, about the time she started attending the Weldon School in 1885.

member of the McCray family told how a doctor was obtained when needed on the South Fork. A rider on a fast horse was sent to Caliente, which was thirty-five miles away and had the nearest phone. A doctor would be called in Bakersfield. He would catch a passenger train, or light engine if there was one available, and rush to Caliente. The Southern Pacific Company made a practice of furnishing this service, gratis, in such an emergency. From Caliente, the doctor was transported the remainder of the journey by a relay of buggies pulled by the fastest teams available. It was almost like the Pony Express. Charles Bennett, who operated a freight outfit out of Caliente, furnished the first team and driver to cover the crooked, steep climb up the Lions Trail and over to Walker Basin. In the Basin, Walker Rankin, Sr., would have a team and driver ready. Changes were also made at John Neil's Hot Springs Ranch and Charles Rankin's Ranch on the South Fork until the doctor reached the sick patient. The horses were driven on the run as the drivers were given orders to use the whip and not spare the horses. One doctor in Bakersfield who was called the most for these emergencies was Dr. Shafer.

A story of one of these trips by Dr. Shafer told how, when the driver almost turned the buggy and passengers over on an especially steep down-hill section, the doctor grabbed the reins. He gave an Indian yell, laid the whip to the team, calling out, "Man, why are you slowing down? Don't you know I am needed at the Powers place?" The story went on to say that in no time they were down the crooked grade with a very frightened ex-driver holding on for dear life.

In 1916, the South Fork Women's Club built a hall at Weldon for community activities. Before this, dances and other functions were held in the South Fork School House. The largest community activities took place at special times such as the 4th of July. There would be a community picnic held along the river in the shade of the willows and cottonwoods. Games and races would be planned for all ages and a platform built for a dance.

In 1892, John McCray decided he wanted to have a ranch of his own. He left Johnnie Johnson, a well known cattleman on the South Fork, as Mr. Landers' foreman, and bought the "Carden Brothers" Ranch six miles west of Weldon. The family fixed up the old Carden house, built about twenty-five years previously. McCray had four or five hundred head of mother cows, which he ran in the

Monache Meadow area in the summertime. He raised alfalfa hay to feed his cattle in the winter; he also raised wheat to sell to Andy Brown, another local rancher. Brown was buying all the surplus grain at seventy cents per hundred to make into flour at his flour mill at Weldon. McCray raised hogs and drove them to Caliente, where he loaded them on railroad cars to be shipped to market. The hogs were bringing one and one-half cents per pound, or about three dollars apiece, delivered in Los Angeles.

A story is told about one herd of hogs being driven from Weldon to Caliente. A snow storm hit the night they arrived in Havilah, which was about half way. They had to remain there for several days while the snow melted. The main problem proved to be not in getting feed to them, but that they pushed several of the houses off their foundations by crawling under the buildings to escape the snow and cold.

Some of the ranchers at Weldon, like the Nicolls, hauled their hogs to Caliente in double-deck freight wagons. Some of the ranchers, after delivering the hogs to the railroad, shoveled the wagons out a little and hauled freight back to the valley.

The Carden Ranch surrounded Rabbit Island, and the flat to the north was known as Carden Flat, before it was named Hanning Flat. A one-room school had been built on the ranch in 1877 and the McCray children attended school there. While living on this ranch, two more daughters were born into the family, Della McCray Campbell in 1895 and Gladys McCray Kofahl in 1896.

In 1898, a severe drought hit. John McCray was lucky enough to be able to sell some of his cattle. He sold one hundred head of his best steers, receiving only ten dollars per head. Although, as most cattlemen, John didn't have any sheep, they were selling for twenty-five cents each that year.

Mr. Landers was not so lucky. His cattle stayed on the range year round and he had to just watch them die off like flies. John's old boss, Mr. Landers, begged him to come back and help him out, so John rented his ranch to his son-in-law, Cecil H. Hanning, and moved his family back to the "Mac Ranch." This was the third time John McCray had worked for Mr. Landers, and this time he stayed four years. During this time, he helped get the Landers Ranch back on a paying basis and then moved back to his home ranch.

By now, the children were all in school, so he moved his family to Bakersfield to have the benefit

Cecil and May Hanning on their wedding day.

of a better school. In 1906, he sold his livestock, rented his ranch, and moved to Bakersfield to be with his family. He went to work for the Kern County Land Company as superintendent of their cattle division. He remained in this job until his death in 1925. His son, Clint, who had started riding with his father when he was just a boy and had worked for Landers and the A. Brown Company as cowboy for awhile, operated the old family ranch before also going to work for the Kern County Land Company in 1924. He took over the job of superintendent upon the death of his father.

While the McCray family was living on the Mac Ranch the second time, the Methodist Church was built across the road from the McCray home. Mr. Livingston, the minister, lived with the McCrays and helped the carpenters build the church. John McCray also helped when he could and Ellen McCray cooked for the crew working on the church. Other ladies also brought food by. After the church was finished, everybody worked to pay off the debt. The women held many church socials. Homemade cakes and ice cream were made and sold. It was said that the big event of the year was a party on

The Landers cattle suffering during the drought of 1898.

Christmas Eve. A beautiful piñon pine tree was brought in and decorated with strings of popcorn and cranberries, and gifts were put under it for all the children.

Cattle ranches such as the one operated by Bill Landers from the 1870's through the 1890's were as different from ranches of today as night and day. The main reason was that Landers ran his herds twelve months of the year on government land. Other large ranchers of that period, such as the Tejon Ranch, Miller and Lux, and Kern County Land Company, depended much more on land they owned outright for grazing.

The General Land Office had been created in 1812 to regulate land use. After California became part of the Union in 1850, the land Landers ran his cattle on should have been regulated by this office. However, it wasn't until the late 1890's that much was done about curtailing the numbers grazing on government land or issuing permits for these privileges.

The area Landers chose for his range when he moved to the South Fork of the Kern River in 1877 covered the Mojave Desert from Little Lake on the north to Antelope Valley on the south, with some of his cattle drifting as far as Victorville.

After the Civil War, the United States government transferred to the Union Pacific and Central Pacific Railroads 200 million acres to assure that they would be able to construct these transcontinental railroad lines. Some of these railroad sections were scattered down the Mojave Desert in the area Landers chose for his new range. He soon purchased 28,000 acres scattered throughout his range, most of it comprised of these railroad sections, with a few school sections included. His range included Kelso Valley and Kelso Canyon, where he purchased choice parcels. Many of these parcels of land had on them the only stock water for miles around, and in this way, he controlled the range by controlling the water. Adjoining the desert land was range at higher elevations, such as Piute and Scodie Mountains. Further south, there were areas of higher elevation where he could move his cattle in the summertime when the feed and water dried up on his desert range.

In the South Fork Valley, Landers first purchased what is now known as the Onyx Ranch and used this as his headquarters. This he purchased from three bachelors by the names of Waterworth, Morgan, and Scott. He also purchased a choice parcel of land from H. L. Mack. Before the flood of 1862, which changed the course of the Kern River, it used to run through this property. There were then, and still are, about 200 acres of choice native pasture. Landers used this large pasture to hold about 2,000 head of big three-year-old steers for three or four weeks until the buyer from Visalia came over to make arrangements to purchase them and to have them delivered to Visalia.

When Landers was on his main spring "works," he employed about twenty cowboys. To mount this size crew, he would have to take on the works with him a seventy or eighty head "remuda." When the wagon wasn't out, Landers didn't keep many horses on the home ranch. When the spring work was finished, which included branding the calves and gathering the beef steers, a big part of the remuda would be taken to the horse range in the Coso Mountains. This range is now the northern part of the China Lake Naval Ordinance Test Station. A few of the young horses that had just been

started that year would be kept for the men to ride in the winter camps. The rest would all have their shoes pulled off in preparation for spending the rest of the summer and winter on the horse range.

There had been wild horses on the range since the 1850's, and in the 1880's, Landers turned eighty registered Morgan mares out with the wild ones. The day before the horses were to go out, a crew of men would go to Cole Springs and camp with Dave Cole, who lived there with his family year round keeping track of the horses and prospecting a little. The next day, the men would have the wild bunch in the area of a horse trap, so when the crew bringing the broke horses from the ranch arrived, they would run the two bunches together. By taking them into the trap, it made it much easier to corral the wild bunch. They would rope and brand all the colts born since the last gather, castrating the male colts. They would then pick about thirty head of four- and five-year-old geldings to break. They didn't break anything younger, as they felt the younger horses didn't have the stamina for the long hard days of work they would be exposed to.

During the last part of May each year, Landers would gather his crew together and get ready for the spring works. Besides his foreman, he kept about six men on during the late summer and winter. They had been staying in line camps out on the range for the past nine months, checking the water and seeing to it that the Landers cattle didn't drift

A group of Landers cowboys pose for the camera on their wiry little mustangs.

too far off their range. The majority of the crew he hired only for the time of spring works. These fifteen men were mostly Indians from the South Fork.

The Indians in the Kern River Valley got their first horses from the missions along the coast about 1800 or earlier. They seemed to be naturally-born horsemen and made some of the finest cowboys in the West.

One of the first rodeos Lander's men held in the Kern River Valley was held just south of Scovern Hot Springs. Mence and Murray had sent their new foreman, Jose Perez, to bring back any of their cattle that had drifted over Greenhorn. John McCray and his crew camped near Jose and his cowboys. The following story was told in later years to John's son, Clint, by Mr. Perez.

"When I saw John and his boys, I really felt sorry for my old friend. His cowboys were Indians, poorly dressed, and their outfits were shabby. They didn't look smart enough to work cattle. My men were Mexicans and white men who wore good clothes and had fine saddles, bridles, and riatas. But when it came to rounding up the strays and renegade cattle (those that got away time after time), it was the Indian cowboys who brought them in every time. My boys couldn't do the work in the rough mountainous country."

A lot of the Indian cowboys who worked for Landers, worked for the A. Brown Company when the Landers wagon wasn't out. They herded sheep out of one of the two sheep camps that Andy Brown operated, or worked in the fields farming with horse and mule teams. When the time of year rolled around for the Landers wagon to go out, the Indi-

Willie Nicoll, a South Fork cowboy in the 1890's.

ans would quit whatever job they were working at and show up ready to go to the desert for the June works.

In the '70's and '80's, many of the Indians didn't have a last name, or at least an English name, and were listed on the books only as Indian Willie, Indian Jack, Indian Henry, or Indian Pedro. One they called Cat Fish Charlie because of his big mouth. Another Indian, known best as Red Eyed Pete, was actually Pete Miranda. Regardless of what name they went by, the Indian cowboys were hard to beat.

The Indian families of Chico, Andreas, and Bencoma each had several generations of cowboys who worked for the Landers Ranch. While they made good hands in all aspects of ranch work, the working of cattle was their first love. Most of them were exceptional trackers and could tell from looking at a bunch of tracks how many cattle had passed, whether they were cows, calves, yearlings, or bulls, and how long ago they had made the tracks. This was a carry-over from the generations of hunting and tracking wild game before the white man came to the valley.

There were always three or four young boys working for Landers, and John McCray's daughter, May, told about some he had to help on their horses because they were too short to reach the stirrups. Ad Cross was one of these young lads, being

Three South Fork cowboys who worked for Landers in the 1880's. From left: Pleas Powers, Alonzo Gibony, and Vic Powers.

**From left: Bob Palmer with Ad Cross at a picnic on Greenhorn Mountain. Both were pioneer cattlemen.**

twelve years old when he came to work for Landers in 1878. Willie Nicoll was only nine years old when he ran away from home and went with the Landers wagon. Willie's dad caught up with them that night and brought him back, but it wasn't long before his parents realized that it did no good to try to discourage him from following the cowboy life. My dad, Marvin Powers, first worked for Landers when he was fifteen, and his brothers, Charlie, Preston, and Jack, all went out with the Landers' wagon at an early age. It seemed as if, from the time the boys on the South Fork were able to climb on their first horse, to ride for the Landers' wagon was their main ambition.

As I mentioned before, it wasn't a full-time job for many of them because most of the year Landers' crew consisted of his foreman and five or six steady men, such as Dave Cole, Johnnie Johnson, Benny Roberts, Bob Thomas, and Jake Prewitt. Other good cowboys who worked for Landers over the years were Mark Lacey, August Glade, Pete Labochotte, Red Vega, Earl McCay, Frank Apalatea, and Earl and Vick Phillips.

When the regular hands went to the desert horse range and brought back the remuda, they started shoeing them and getting the wagon ready to leave. Many of the men who had been working at other

jobs for eight or nine months showed up at the Mack Ranch ready to go out with the wagon. The chuck wagon, with a bed wagon along sometimes, would head south, camping the first night at the Kelso Valley line camp. The twenty or so cowboys would ride along with some of the younger hands, driving the horse herd of 70 to 80. The second night out, many times they camped on the outskirts of the little railroad town of Mojave. Twenty or so cowboys turned loose in town overnight usually livened things up considerably. Several times, one or two of the cowboys had to be hauled along in the chuck wagon the next morning until they could operate on their on steam. When the chuck wagon reached the southern part of the range down around Antelope Valley, the work would start.

Once the work started, the remuda would have to be herded night and day, and this job always fell to one of the youngsters. Ad Cross started his cowboying by watching the horse herd, and his son, Clifford, told me the following story about this job his dad was given as horse wrangler. Ad, who was just twelve when he started, got his sleep in short snatches between his job of keeping track of 80 or so horses and keeping the cook supplied with wood. Clifford told how Ad was given a mule to use each night as he took the horse herd out to graze. He would tie his blankets behind the saddle, and

**Frank Apalatea, as a young man, riding for Bill Landers. Frank rode for all the owners of this ranch for half a century.**

**Ad Cross and his son, Jim.**

Clifford Cross, Jr. as he worked for the Onyx Ranch in the 1950's. He was the third generation of his family to cowboy on this ranch. Clifford also worked for the ZX Ranch in Oregon. He agreed with the author that they had the roughest horses in the West.

Clifford Cross, a man who not only cowboyed in the Kern River Valley, but also for several ranchers in Arizona, New Mexico, and on the historic Miller and Lux Ranch in the San Joaquin Valley.

after getting his charges settled on good feed, he would tie his mule to a Joshua Tree and roll up in his blankets. He related later that he never did have any trouble going to sleep. There was just one mare in the bunch, and she had a bell. The horses, as a rule, would follow this bell mare. If the horses drifted too far away and the mule couldn't hear the bell, he would start pawing, braying, and raising such a ruckus that Ad would wake up, saddle his mule and ride off to find the wandering horses, sometimes in pitch dark. He would find them and bring them back to where they were supposed to be, roll up in his blankets, and go back to sleep. He never had any trouble finding them as the mule would put his nose to the ground and track them like a bloodhound, even on the darkest night.

Clifford Cross and his twin brother, Claude, also worked for Landers in 1918. Clifford's son, Clifford, Jr., also cowboyed on the same ranch in the 1950's when Rudnick and Alexander owned it.

When the work started on the southern part of the range, the local cattlemen in the area, such as the Cuddebacks, would throw in with the Landers wagon, which furnished the grub for the whole outfit. Landers, in return, branded all the "big ears" (calves who had left their mothers) with his "L" brand. These animals, most of them yearlings or older, couldn't really be called calves, but had quit following their mothers and there was no way of knowing who they belonged to.

The chuck wagon cook was a big part of the early cattle business, and his word was law in the vicinity of his cooking fire. Even the cowboss very seldom disputed his work, and the cow hands—especially the younger members of the roundup—walked mighty lightly in the area of his domain.

Once in awhile, someone might remark that the gravy was mighty salty, but would quickly add, "But that's just the way I like it." These cooks had a big job. Often they had a helper, but many times they would feed from fifteen to thirty men twice a day, in addition to moving the wagon every day or so and setting up camp again. Some of the cooks included Shorty Burnett, Phil Seybert, and Ed Gessell.

The meals eaten out of a tin pan while sitting on their bedroll by a sagebrush fire, made either favorable or unfavorable impressions on most of the old time cowboys. A cook that most remember was Louie Bowers, and here again, different cowboys had different impressions of his culinary skills. Frank Apalatea said Louie was the "best cook I ever saw; always had hot grub whenever you came in, day or night." Pete Labachotte, on the other hand, was not so impressed with Louie, and noted that he was the "dirtiest cook I ever saw; spit right

Louie Bowers, the controversial cook on the Landers Chuck Wagon, in his later years.

across the frying pan—didn't make it every time, either. You know, one time I cut a stink bug right in two in the bread."

At best, the cooking conditions were anything but ideal. If the cook had a small table that hooked up to the tailgate of the wagon, he was lucky. Everything else had to be done on the ground. Different cooks might favor certain types of cooking, but most of them followed the same procedure in setting up their cooking area. Generally, a six foot pit would be dug about a foot wide and eight inches deep. Greasewood was used mainly for fuel in the desert, and was hard to beat for cooking. When the fire had burned down to a three-inch bed of coals, you had a good, even heat that would last long enough to cook a meal. Some of the cooking was done on rods laid crossways over the fire pit, but most of it was done by sticking iron stakes in the ground vertically, on which another rod would be placed horizontally. From this, the cooking vessels would hang with the aid of fire hooks, "short iron" rods crooked in the opposite direction at each end. The cooking equipment numbered four or five frying pans and as many Dutch ovens, a few kettles, and the ever present coffee pot. The Dutch oven (a large cast iron pot with a rim on the lid to hold the coals) was the most used of any of the cooking paraphernalia.

Bread was baked for each meal and, to the cowboy, nothing would measure up to sourdough bread. The cook had his sourdough keg or crock, which he guarded with his life. This keg usually held about three gallons.

The sourdough batch was started by simply placing in the crock, flour, salt, and enough water to make a medium-thick batter. When this was well stirred, it was put in a warm place for a couple of days to ferment. The good sourdough cooks said that you had to use sourdough at least twice a day to make it work the best. At each meal, the cook would take out enough sourdough to make his bread, then add enough salt, flour, and water to always have plenty of working batter.

In making his bread, he added to the sourdough batter more flour, a little soda, salt, and a generous amount of lard. After making sure that the soda and lard were thoroughly mixed in, he would pinch off pieces the size of an egg. These were then coated with hot grease and placed as close to each other as possible in a preheated Dutch oven, as this made them lighter by rising more. The full oven was then placed beside the fire for about half an hour to rise. The cook put them on the coals at just the right time with a generous supply of coals on the lid so that this would finish cooking when the rest of the meal was done, as sourdough biscuits are best eaten hot.

Much of the mystery that surrounds a good sourdough cook comes from his knowledge of the right temperature to keep his working batter, and the fact that he used it at least twice a day. Most of the time, the rest was just years of practice, and no recipe ever handed down seemed to get the results that those old boys achieved.

Even higher on the cowboy's list of necessities was his coffee, and the pot of about three-gallon size was always on the fire. The cowboy liked his coffee strong, and the usual recipe was a handful of coffee for each cup of water. The sight of the wide-bottomed, smoke-blackened coffee pot on the coals, with the brown boiling liquid overflowing down its sides, was a picture that would make the cowboy's mouth water. Although he drank huge quantities of this potent brew, it never seemed to keep him awake at night.

The first wagons that went out had on their bill of fare only meat, bread, and coffee; then later, beans were added, and the usual sight when the meal was being prepared was a black iron pot with cooking beans bubbling in it over the coals, which would whet the appetite of any man. In later years, potatoes were used almost at every meal, and the wagon cook also started using canned goods. Canned tomatoes were the most popular, but some vegetables, such as peas and corn, were also used.

Plenty of good, desert-raised beef was killed on the spot whenever the supply on hand ran out. They didn't age the beef as they do now, but started eating it the day after it was killed. Much of the beef was fried, but stew got its share. Most often on the menu were plenty of boiled potatoes, although fried potatoes were common. The ever-present pink beans were included, as were peas or corn. Gravy that was made in the frying pan after the meat was cooked accompanied most meals. Sourdough bread, cooked in a dutch oven, and coffee usually rounded out the meal, unless some type of dried fruit was cooked up for dessert. These were the simplest of diets, but they seemed to stick to the ribs. It kept the cowboys going about their daily work, which was anything but light.

As any army marches on its mess kitchens, the cowboy works on his chuck wagon. Sometimes the cook would have a canvas fly hooked to the back of the wagon, but it usually wasn't enough to keep the blazing sun from baking his back and shoulders or the cold rain from soaking him. Regardless of all the drawbacks—wind that blew sand in the food, a shortage of wood, and a limited variety of foodstuffs on which to draw—these old boys still left reputations behind them that are hard to top. The type of riding done by these cowboys called for top physical condition, and those who did not have the needed vitality soon fell by the way.

Besides the two or three regular meals each day, the cook was expected to have something for the crew to eat when they went on duty for night herding (the herding was mandatory since there were no fences). The night was divided between two shifts, and all hands took their turn. When the men went on at midnight, a pot of beans or stew and plenty of coffee were kept warm by the fire so they could fill up before going out.

Each morning just about dawn, the chuck wagon would come alive with activity. The cook had been up an hour or more working by lantern light, starting breakfast. The following was typical of this most colorful scene. The wrangler had just run the horses into a rope corral. This consisted of only one rope being held waist high by the cowboys, as each man took his turn entering and roping his horse for the day. They were led to an area close to the chuck wagon where horses had been unsaddled the day before. As each man saddled his horse, the picture livened up considerably. Things started to happen. Out of twenty or more horses being ridden that day, there were always at least two or three that wanted nothing to do with the saddle. Even after being hobbled, they might tear up half an acre of ground before they were able to be saddled and made ready to go. As the men started to mount and get their broncs lined out for the day's work, what you were apt to see is mirrored in one of Charlie Russell's paintings, "Bronc at Breakfast Time," where a cowboy is riding a bucking horse through camp, scattering things right and left. There was a lot of cursing and shouted threats from the cook, but he knew, as everyone else did, that there was no turning or directing a bucking horse. This was the high point of the day for many of the cowboys as they offered shouts of encouragement to the rider, and maybe a hat or two sailed under the bronc to encourage him. If the undetermined route happened to take them through a bunch of yucca, it would get a big laugh from all hands, and several days of discomfort for the luckless rider as the punctures ran their course.

As the sun popped over the Superstition Mountains, the cowboys headed off in groups of five or six to where they split up to work the country scheduled for that day. Everyone knew what was expected; however, the cowboss issued a few brief instructions about who went where.

As the day wore on, cattle started streaming into the predetermined rodeo ground, and by late morning, all the riders had been accounted for.

Many times, the wrangler would bring the remuda out and fresh horses would be caught for the rest of the work. A branding fire was built off to one side. Those calves belonging to the smaller cattlemen, such as the Cuddebacks, would be roped and branded first. When all these were accounted for, the rest—along with any "big ears"—would be branded for Landers. Once in a while, while branding the Landers calves, one of the men would sing out, "Points up," meaning the points of the "L" brand put on the left hip had to be pointing up or the brand would be upside down. Branding was hot, dusty work; however, it was looked forward to, as it gave the men a chance to show their skill with a reata.

When all the branded calves had trotted back to their mothers with smarting hides, cutting of the beef cattle began. Again, a lot of the men would rather cut cattle than eat. As with the branding, much of the success in putting on a good show and getting the job done quickly depended a great deal on the horse they were riding. These little mustangs took naturally to cow work and a man had to have a deep seat in the saddle and many times grab the saddlehorn to stay with them as they dodged and turned to cut out the older steers. In many cases, these steers had horn spreads of over five feet and weighed more than the horse. They had become rolling fat on the desert wild flowers, and the sun glistening off their multicolored hides made these creatures a sight to behold.

With the branding and cutting of the beef finished, the main herd was turned loose to scatter onto the range. The "cut," or beef cattle, were driven back to camp and included with those that had been cut during the previous days.

As the work progressed, the herd of beef steers continued to grow, meaning each night quite a few men had to take turns standing guard for two or three hours. Also, they had to give them a chance to graze enough each day to keep their weight stable. By the time the crew came through Kelso Valley and down to the "Mack" Ranch Meadow, there would be two to three thousand fat three-year-old steers. When they came into the lush meadow, they would string out for more than two miles.

Each summer, as water became scarce and the desert feed dried up, these cattle were "stirred up and started towards the hills." These cows, having run on the same range for years, would travel from thirty to forty miles to the foothills or to their summer range. This included Kelso Valley, the Piutes, and Scodie Mountains. In November or December, they would be pushed back out into the desert. This system did not always work. There are quite a few years recorded when, because of lack of rain, there was hardly a blade of grass on either the mountain or desert range. In years such as 1898, when after six months, John McCray finally finished the count on Landers cattle, he found there were only 2,000 head left from the 20,000 head on the range a year before. The old timers said it was really a sickening sight; that you could ride for miles and never get the stench of rotting cattle out of your nostrils. Some ask why they did not drive them to feed or ship feed their way. In those days, a big steer would bring only seven or eight dollars. Even if you could find feed, the cost would have been prohibitive. All the cattlemen could do was borrow a little money, if possible, to buy beans and pay their riders for the following year, tighten their belts a couple of notches, and hope the next few years would bring them out of debt.

During the 1880's and '90's, a buyer by the name of Mr. Bliss from Visalia came to the "Mack" Ranch where he and Mr. Landers got together on a price which was usually eighteen to twenty dollars apiece upon delivery in Visalia by McCray. The money would be paid in gold coin and brought back in the chuck wagon. Many times John McCray would bring back as much as $40,000 dollars in gold coin. There were never any holdups. It was related that if there was danger of McCray being robbed, a Glennville cattleman by the name of Ned Conner would alert the other cattlemen and officers in the vicinity and some of them would ride along with McCray until the money was safely delivered to Mr. Landers. Mr. Landers, as many of the early pioneers, didn't believe in banks and kept his money in a barrel in his storehouse beside his potatoes and beans. He always used gold coins to pay his help, which, during the 1880's and 1890's, was about one dollar a day plus board. In later years, the cattle would be driven up past Bodfish and Havilah and down through Caliente to Bakersfield, where they were delivered to the slaughterhouse.

After Bill Landers died in 1923, his ranch was leased for several years by Frank Boyce, and then it was purchased by Jack Doyle. Doyle hired Jim Black as cattle foreman and brought a crew of cowboys in from Arizona. After making a variety of changes with the farming operation, as well as the methods of running cattle on the desert range, he decided he wasn't making any money and sold the Landers Ranch to Roland Hill and Oscar Rudnick.

Hill and Rudnick fell out after six or eight months, and Art Alexander, who had been the ranch foreman for the A. Brown Company for twenty-seven years, bought Hill's interest. Alexander and Rudnick operated the ranch for the next twenty-six years. On Alexander's retirement, Rudnick bought his part of the business.

When Roland Hill came to the South Fork Valley, he brought a crew of cowboys from the Bear Mountain Ranch near Tehachapi. Two of these were Farrel and Wink (Bill) Chappell. Farrel's boy, also named Bill and called Windy, came over from Tehachapi and went to work for Alexander and Rudnick as a cowboy in 1932. Windy had been riding colts and working cattle since he was fourteen. After punching cows for awhile, he became the mechanic for the Onyx Ranch, only riding when they needed an extra hand around the feed lot. In

**Bill Chappell, Sr. top horse trainer for Hill Ranch in the 1920's.**

1946, Windy went to work for the State of California on the highway crew at Weldon.

Johnny and Danny Chappell also rode for the Onyx Ranch. Ed Chappell, a brother of Windy, worked for Rudnick and Alexander for many years. In 1955, on Alexander's retirement, Rudnick bought his share of the ranch. When Rudnick took the ranch over, he laid the whole crew of cowboys off and brought in his own crew. At that time, Ed Chappell went to work for the highway department. Wink Chappell, after working on the Onyx Ranch for twenty-four years, much of the time in charge of the whole cattle operation, was also laid off in 1955 by Rudnick. He went up the road one mile and worked for Stanley Smith for thirteen years. Leonard Alexander and Dwight Pascoe, who had been on the Onyx payroll as cowboys for quite a few years, were also laid off by Rudnick, and in 1987, were both still working for the Cal Trans Highway Department. It seems a lot of cowboys I knew went from punching cows to highway work. I know there was no comparison in wages, as a cowboy gets the lowest wages of any working man.

Oscar Rudnick, who many affectionately called "The Old Man," was, to me, one of the most unusual men I have ever known. As a boy growing up, I remember seeing Oscar as he supervised the weighing and shipping of steers from his feed lot at Onyx. It made a big impression on me because he seemed to show the same deference and respect to everyone. Even after his various businesses furnished employment for five hundred persons with a yearly payroll of nearly three million dollars, he continued to take a personal interest in each employee. I also remember seeing him in his striped overalls taking care of the many details around the Kern Valley Packing Plant. He once surprised the men who worked in the boning room by jumping in and helping out on a busy day, and he was able to keep up with the best of them.

Oscar immigrated from Lithuania (now Russia) in 1906 when he was fourteen. Because he disliked the East, he came to California and became a salesman of Watkins Products, traveling with a horse and buggy. His route took him to eastern California and western Nevada. As he traveled from ranch to ranch, he also traded in horses.

Later, he made his headquarters in the town of McFarland, where he would butcher livestock under a tree at night and peddle it early the next morning to the farmers and ranchers in the area. In

1911, he married Libbie Berman of Los Angeles, and after a few years of owning a grocery store in the southland, his interest in livestock brought him back to Bakersfield in 1919.

He first worked for Mr. Sol Coleman, who owned the Kern Valley Packing Company on the Kern Island Road. He finally bought the packing plant. At that time, the plant consisted of only a small room with a board floor and was only big enough to hold five beef carcasses. Because there was no electricity to operate refrigeration, the beef was butchered at night and sold first thing in the morning. There was a small frame house nearby, and it was here he housed his growing family. His wife not only cooked for their family, but also for the men working in the plant. The packing plant grew until it eventually processed beef, sausage, smoked meats, bacon, lamb and pork.

In 1925, Oscar branched out into the cattle business. One of his early acquisitions was in 1932 when he bought the Onyx Ranch from Jack J. Doyle, the prizefight promoter. He bought the original 28,000 acres in partnership with A. J. Alexander. Other parcels of land were added later until the Onyx Ranch, in 1987, consisted of 167,000 acres in fee, and also controlled 153,000 acres in government lands and private leases. In normal years, the ranch ran about 5,000 head of steers.

Later, the Rudnick Trust Feed Yard was acquired, which, in the 1960's, was the largest independent feedlot operating in Kern County. In 1950, the Piute Packing Company was bought by the Rudnick Trust Estate and it was a major supplier of the Armed Forces.

Between the years of 1936 and 1940, Oscar Rudnick, with his various partners in the sheep business, ran about 150,000 breeding ewes. They ranged from Yerington, Nevada to Palm Springs, California. After 1941, the sheep operation was cut down because of the labor shortage. During the early 1950's, Oscar fed about 45,000 head of cattle yearly in his own feedlots and ran about 15,000 head of cattle on his various ranches.

It is said that Oscar Rudnick had more partners than anyone in the history of Kern County. Some of his business ventures included the M & R Sheep Co., Eureka Livestock Co., Antelope Cattle and Milling Co., Corn Fed Cattle Co., El Tejon Cattle Co., Chanley Brothers Trucking, International Feed and Fertilizer Co., Cloverhead Sheep Co., Ox Cattle Co., Brea Valley Processing Co., and the Imperial Land and Cattle Co.

His daughter, Sophie Rudnick, who put together much of the material I am using, said she thought the reason he had so many partners was, "Because he liked people and believed in them, and also was a man of exceptional vision and could see opportunities which others passed by."

Sophie also told how her father surprised the cattlemen in Mono County when they received a supplementary check to the price they had already collected for their cattle. Her father had written them that he had made more money than he had expected on their cattle and wished to share the extra profit with them. His philosophy was, "No deal is a good deal unless it is good on both sides."

In 1945, Rudnick bought the Three V Ranch (VVV) in northern Arizona, with the headquarters in Seligman. The ranch consisted of 950,000 acres, bordered on the south by the Hualpai Indian Reservation and on the east by Highway 64. During the period from 1945 to 1950, Oscar and his son, Marcus, ran this operation. This ranch, which ran as many as 27,000 head of cattle at one time, still had chuck wagons pulled by teams. It sold to the Kern County Land Company in 1950. In 1987, another Rudnick was one of the leasers of the Three V Ranch. This was Richard, Oscar's grandson. The ranch was raising registered Brayford

**Marcus Rudnick in the 1950's. He always rode at a fast trot or a lope.**

**One of the Rudnick herds on the 3V Ranch, in the 1940's. This herd had 2,500 hereford cows and they had just put 250 Brahman bulls in with them. This was some of their first cross breeding.**

Top hand, Les Jenkins, saddling his mare, Blondie. He was working for Rudnick at this time.

Oscar Rudnick with his second wife, Sophie, and their daughter, Rebecca. Christmas 1952.

bulls produced from using registered gray Brahman bulls on a herd of registered Hereford cows.

All five of his sons worked in the family businesses at various times. His sons, Marcus, Sam, Milton, and Philip have served as trustees of the Rudnick Estates Trust.

Libbie Rudnick, who bore him eleven children, passed away on February 23, 1951. On August 5, 1951, Oscar Married Dr. Sophie Loven Goldman, and a daughter, Rebecca Sophie, was born on November 20, 1952. Oscar made good on a prediction he made as a youth that one day he would have twelve children and a million dollars.

After 1949, failing health had caused Oscar to designate more of his business to his sons, but because his work was his avocation, as well as his vocation, he could not give it up entirely. Two days before he passed away on September 23, 1959, his oldest daughter, Bertha Sklar, asked, "Papa, why do you work so hard?" He answered, "My child, because I love it."

Like many good business men, Oscar was wise in picking people to fill key jobs. Of the many super employees he had over the years, the one remembered best was his right hand man, Mark Charles Parks. Over the thirty-nine years Parks worked for Rudnick, he served in many capaci-

ties such as buying and selling livestock and ranch manager.

On October 25, 1969, when Mark Parks was honored as Cattleman of the Year for the Kern Branch of the California Cattlemens Association, Mrs. Robert (Alice) Beard, president of the Kern County Cow Belles, gave the introduction. She

Mark Parks, the only man to receive an open checkbook from Oscar Rudnick.

spoke of Parks as "Being to the livestock industry what Aaron is to baseball, Hayes is to the theater, Hope is to comedy, or Unitas is to football." She went on to say, "No other person in the Western United States knows more about livestock, not only cattle, but the entire field of livestock, than does Mark Parks. He understands cattle, sheep, horses, hogs, and yes—dogs. He understands the feeding, training, doctoring, handling, and marketing of all these animals."

Mark was born in 1889 in San Jose, Santa Clara County, California. In 1909, he went to Chihuahua, Mexico, where he ran the Santana Division of the million acre San Jose de Barbicora Rancho for Mrs. William Randolph Hearst. This was one of the three divisions on the ranch.

On this ranch where his father had been before him, Mark became acquainted with the notorious Pancho Villa. In 1916, Villa was losing control, and although he had promised Mark he would never be killed, Parks decided to run for his life, making a quick exit from Mexico on a railroad handcar.

In California, Parks went to San Francisco, where he got a job for Miller and Lux. Henry Miller had been retired for six years at this time and died the year Parks went to work for the company. When Parks asked J. Leroy Nickel, who had married Henry's daughter, Nellie, for a job, Nickel said, "You mean a position!" Parks' reputation had preceded him, for while he was in Mexico, he had once purchased 10,000 head of steers for Miller and Lux.

Parks first ran the Firebough Division for Miller and Lux, which, at that time, had 25,000 head of mother cows. There was an infestation of Texas fever on the ranch and Parks succeeded in cleaning it up. He received a raise every month for the first twelve months of his employment. In 1917, he was transferred to the Southern Division at Buttonwillow where Miller and Lux ran an additional 52,000 mother cows. His main assignment was to buy out the sheepmen. He remained there until the 1920's when Elmer Houchin Interest took over.

During the brief time he worked for the Cholane Cattle Co., he met Jeannie Patriquin, who later became Mrs. Mark Parks. The four sons from this union are Mark, Jr., Gale, Arch, and Bill.

In 1923, Parks began what was to be thirty-nine years of service with Oscar Rudnick and his heirs. Walker Rankin, Jr., who was a man of few words, said of Mark Parks, "He is a fine judge of cattle; a fine cow buyer; the best! Yes, he is a champion." And he truly was.

In the Kern River Valley, in 1987, Oscar Rudnick's dream was still going strong. The Rudnicks were still operating the Onyx Ranch; a grandson, Richard Rudnick, flies in periodically, landing on

The Marcus Rudnick family in 1965. From left: Ben, John, Lisa, Roberta with Wendy, Marcus with Bronco, Marcia, Joe, Millie, Libbie, Jennifer, and Richard.

The Onyx store in 1987. Built in 1880 this historic store on Highway 178 is operated by Ben Rudnick and his family. It has always been a popular spot where valley cowboys hang out.

The Rudnick crew gather at the Onyx store for a cup of coffee before starting the day. From the left: Buddy Montes, Lori Montes, Wynona and Tippy Tipton, and in the back, Carol McDonald.

Lefty Dennison, long-time ranch foreman for Rudnick on the Onyx Ranch.

the old Mack Ranch meadow where Landers sold his longhorn steers to the buyers. Richard divides his time between running the cattle on the Onyx Ranch and his other interests, such as the Three V Ranch in Arizona. Bennie Rudnick, another grandson, manages the farming on the ranch and operates the historic Onyx Store.

Those who were in charge of the farming operation over the years knew their business, too. Some of these were Glenn Alexander, who was a foreman for Alexander and Rudnick, Eddie Coughran III, and Lefty Dennison, who later were foremen for Rudnick. I also think of men like Sid Weldon, who I feel usually does the work of three men and was still farming on the Onyx Ranch in 1987.

In the year 1987, Tip Tipton, Sr. and Tip Tipton, Jr. were the main cowboys working for the Onyx Ranch with Tip, Jr's. wife, Wynona, working as extra help when they needed her. Her sister, Carol McDonald, also worked as needed. I would put Tip, Jr., his brother Buckshot, and Jimmy McDonald, who all work cattle in the Kern River Valley, up against any other three cowboys working any kind of cattle in any type of country. The two

The Onyx Ranch crew outside the saddle house. At left: Carol McDonald with her two daughters, Katie (left) and Raina, Buddy Montes, Wynona Tipton, Tip Tipton, Sr. with his two boys, Buckshot and Tippy. (Photo by Casey Christie.)

Old time cowboys together for a barbecue in 1987. From left: Tip Tipton, Sr., Dutch Henderson, Bob **Powers (in the black hat), John McNally, Buzzy Palmer, Glenn Alexander, and Ken Rhoads.** (Photo by Casey Christie.)

A group of old timers who worked on the Onyx Ranch. From left: Bob Powers, Ken Rhoads, Buzzy Palmer, Dutch Henderson, Clifford Cross, and Glenn Alexander. (Photo by Casey Christie)

wives, Carol and Wynona, are also top hands with a lot of cow sense.

Tip Tipton, Sr., who was raised on the Tejon Ranch, was, in 1987, still camped at the same cow camp and living with his wife in the same line shack that John McCray moved into with his wife and baby in 1880.

Tip Tipton, Sr's. dad had also worked cattle in the San Joaquin Valley for Ferdinand A. Tracy near Bakersfield, and also for the Miller and Lux Ranch. The Tipton family have definitely been cowboys to the very core for the past three generations.

# Cattle on the Open Range

As I grew up on the South Fork of the Kern River, I became deeply steeped in the tradition of ranch life. For three generations my family had been in the cattle business in that location. One of my great-grandfathers, Thomas H. Smith, had brought a small herd of cattle with him in 1861 when he settled near Onyx. In 1852, another great-grandfather, John W. Powers, settled in Mendocino County, bringing with him from Missouri "a large drove of cattle." In 1874, he and his family moved their operation to Riverside County. Of John's twelve children, most of his eight sons grew up working cattle on the open range.

In the late 1870's, John Powers' boys met some of the men from the Landers Ranch, as they worked the same range on the Mojave River. In 1879, one of these boys, James H. Powers, came to the South Fork. After working for Landers one year, he married the daughter of Thomas H. and Sophia Smith and went into the cattle business for himself.

Victor Powers, an early California cowboy in the 1880's.

In eighteen years, there were fourteen children born to him and Henrietta. Four of these sons, Charles, Preston, Jack, and my dad, Marvin P. Powers, all became top hands. Jack and Marvin spent their whole lives in the cattle business.

My dad quit school and started riding for the A. Brown Co. when he was fourteen years old, and later rode for Bill Landers. He served in the army during World War I, and when he was discharged, he bought the Old Johnson Ranch on the South Fork. In the same year, he obtained his first permit to run cattle in the Sequoia National Forest in the

Thomas and Sophia Smith. Sophia was the first white woman to live on the South Fork.

James Henry Powers in 1880.

Jack Powers, a cowboy all his life.

summer. Soon after, he was granted a permit to graze his cattle on the Mojave Desert in the winter and spring.

In 1919, Marvin, Sr. and his wife, Isabel, moved into the Old Johnson house that was fifty years old at the time, and lived there for the next thirty years. After they moved down the road a couple of miles, my two brothers, Marvin, Jr., and Bill, and I all started our married life in this old home.

During the years between the 1920's and the 1950's, there were many more lean years than there were good ones. Marvin, Sr. and his family, at times, barely hung on to their little ranch by the skin of their teeth. Marvin took a job as State Cattle Inspector in the Kern River Valley, and the small salary many times was all that kept food on the table. This meant that during the summer, when the cattle were in the high country, my dad had to stay on the home ranch much of the time so he would be available to inspect cattle as they were shipped out of the valley. A big part of his job was inspecting the beef steers as they were taken out of the feed lot at the Onyx Ranch and shipped to the slaughter house in Bakersfield.

Marvin Powers, Jr., sits in the doorway of the storehouse at the old Powers Ranch, holding the family Circle Dot brand.

The Powers family camped at Powell Meadow (originally Powers Meadow) in 1932. From left: Marvin, Sr., Bill, Isabel, Bob, and in front, Marvin, Jr.

When my two brothers and I were small, my dad would move his family the fifty miles to the summer camp with pack mules and leave us there with my mother. All three of us grew up with a love of the high country we spent each summer in, fishing, hunting for Indian arrowheads, and playing in the lush meadows.

My mother wasn't raised in a cow camp, so there were many things that came up that must have made her wonder at her decision to marry a westerner. When the black bears would visit our camp

The Powers family in the High Sierra in 1931. From left: Bob on Peanut, Isabel holding Bill on Jim Pinto, Marvin, Sr. on Cowboy, and Marvin, Jr. on Blackbird.

at night and the coyotes would keep up a racket most nights, the walls of the tent must not have seemed very secure. The summer thunderstorms, with the lightning striking the trees on the ridge above camp, and the sudden downpour that followed, I know gave her many tense moments. The nearest neighbor was Lloyd Allen, a forest ranger at Beach Meadow. This was five miles away by horseback and he wasn't there all the time. The closest road was twenty miles away at Kennedy Meadows.

In these years while I was growing up, I missed something that is really important. That was working cattle day after day with someone who was a good teacher. As I mentioned before, my dad, because he had to be at the home ranch inspecting cattle, wasn't there to give the individual attention that many times makes the difference between a youngster really learning to work cattle the proper way or just being able to barely get by. The young person who grows up working beside someone who is a natural teacher, someone who really wants to see the next generation grow up being even better handlers of livestock than themselves, is indeed fortunate.

I hear cowboys talk about being raised on a

Bob Powers on Cedar, a top cow horse, in 1940.

67

ranch with somebody like Tony Araujo, who was the cowboss for the Tejon Company. They say Tony was always helping the younger hands and encouraging them to excel without being critical.

The first one I remember riding with that tried to help me put together a better method of breaking colts was Wink Chappell. Wink was a natural born teacher and not only helped me, but a lot of other young people in the Kern River Valley. By this time, I was twenty-four years old and orthopedic problems were starting to curtail my cowboying. I really loved breaking colts, but I guess you could say the "spirit was willing, but the flesh was weak."

In later years, Wink moved to Ridgecrest, California, where he had a total of two hundred pupils during his years of teaching at his riding school. He was a top trainer, and in 1976, Ibn Nasha, a full blooded Arabian gelding that he broke and showed, was the second best gelding in the state of California in the Western Working Class.

There are things that people who have been around stock all their lives do automatically, like constantly "reading the cattle." Rather than just hollering at a young hand and telling him to wake up when a cow breaks out of the herd on the side the youngster is holding, these old timers would explain to him that if you will watch the herd closely, you can tell ahead of time when an animal is going to try to make a break for it. If the youngster is riding a good cow horse, instead of the plugs like I

Wink Chappell on Ibn Nasha, a full-blooded Arabian gelding that he broke. Together they placed second best gelding in California in the Western Working Class in 1976.

grew up on, the horse does a lot of the watching for him. A good horse also helps in a green hand's understanding of how to work cattle. If a horse dodges out from under him once or twice, you can bet he will pay attention. He should learn to keep his eyes constantly moving, watching the people cutting the herd, so he will know what animals are to go out, glancing behind him to see that the cut (those already cut out) don't try to run back into the herd. There are things to be explained to him such as, why you never go into a herd and help part out cattle unless you are told to do so by the boss, and that you keep your position on a cattle drive or while holding cattle unless you are told to move by the boss. Sometimes, you might have to leave your position to help someone, but you are expected to return to it as soon as possible.

Most people who have been around cattle most of their lives instinctively resent anyone mistreating cattle, whether theirs or someone else's. The young hand will learn that it is best to get his roping practice in the roping arena rather than in the open or on a cattle drive. It not only makes the animals wild, but runs weight off them.

There are basic principles to learn about driving a herd for any distance. If these things are explained as they come up, the youngster will learn much faster; things such as, cattle work just like a syphon, and if they get strung out too far and can't see the cattle ahead, you are losing the benefit of your leaders. The ones in front that want to travel will more or less encourage the cattle following them. If you have to take a small bunch to get through a rough place where the cattle aren't moving through, you take only a few ahead until they start traveling good again. The riders in the lead generally hold up the leaders if they get too far ahead and the herd starts to become separate bunches.

There are a multitude of things for the young rider to learn, and if she or he has someone explaining the whys and hows of the business, it sometimes makes the difference in whether he or she will ever be classed as a top hand or not.

The following pages were written for one of my previous books, *South Fork Country.* When I wrote down these thoughts, I hadn't been closely associated with the Fish Creek Range since the family sold the ranch and permit in 1952. I wrote this in 1968 and, at that time, I was Range Officer on the Fish Creek Allotment for the U.S. Forest Service. As I started to write *Cowboy Country,* I wanted to include this time period of my life, but when I started to rewrite this chapter, it just wouldn't come out right. The feeling of homesickness or nostalgia I felt the first time I wrote it helped me to produce an account I couldn't match some twenty years later. I hope those who have read *South Fork Country* will enjoy re-reading this chapter.

Starting in the 1920's, Marvin Powers, Sr., ran cattle on the same winter and summer range with four other cattlemen and their families. Stanley Smith, a cousin, ran his cattle operation from the ranch his grandfather, Thomas H. Smith, founded in 1861. Stanley and his wife, Gwen, were helped by their two daughters, Joyce and Loraine, who both learned to ride soon after they started walking.

In 1987, Joyce and her husband, Buzz Shaw, were operating their cattle business from the Bloomfield Ranch located a mile east of the old Smith Ranch. Anyone who has handled cattle very much has known men or women who have a photographic memory for animals they have worked. Joyce is one of these people. In pairing up cows and calves I believe she is one of the best. In 1987 Loraine Smith Bailey was still running cattle on her great-grandfather's ranch and family permits with a partner, Jim Neukirchner. Loraine always rode good horses, and rough country and wild cattle are right up her alley.

The third man in this quartet was Bill Alexander. Bill married Isabel Powers' sister, Dorothy, and their two children, Lois and Keith, worked the ranch with their parents. In 1987 Keith's children, Kim and Kit, were operating the Alexander Ranch.

Stanley Smith, Range Boss on the Fish Creek Range in the 1960's.

Branding at Broder Meadow in the High Sierras 1945. From left: Leonard Alexander, Bob Powers, Joyce Smith Shaw, filling vaccine gun, Harvey Robinson, Fred Burke and Loraine Smith Bailey roping on Star. In foreground Ray Milligan dehorning and Bill Powers getting ready apply pine-tar after the job is done.

The fourth cattleman was Jim Robertson. Jim married Bill Alexander's sister, Ann. Their daughter, Evelyn, grew up on the ranch and kept the grazing permits after her father retired. A nephew, Leonard Alexander, worked cattle on the desert and mountain range for his Uncle Jim for over twenty years and knew this range and how the cattle should be worked as well as anyone who had ridden there before. By the 1960's Dr. Norman Sprague had purchased the Powers and Robertson permits and was still operating them in the late 1980's.

In the 1940's, the winter range on the Mojave Desert was divided in the following manner: Alexander and Robertson had the southern section of what was called the Walker's Pass Common Allotment. Powers had the next portion, or range, and Smith Ranch had the northern-most part of the range. On the summer range, all four cattlemen ran on the same range, known as the Fish Creek Allotment.

Early in the Alexander-Robertson-Powers-Smith association, it became apparent that Stanley Smith had the rare ability to manage men tactfully, patiently, and firmly. It was agreed among the other three that Stanley should be rodeo boss of the cattle operation. So appointed, he began this position in 1920. The rodeo boss had the final say-so regarding cattle on the summer range and the drives to and from the range. A certain amount of discussion was allowed concerning how and when to work the cattle, but the daily plan of work and the final decisions were the responsibility of the rodeo boss. Stanley Smith handled the job ably.

Few changes in operation methods had been made over the years until the early 1950's. Few were necessary. The early settlers who followed the Indian trails into the mountain meadows soon learned the secrets of making the most of their range land. The hard-earned knowledge has been passed down from generation to generation. Formation of the Forest Service in the early 1900's curtailed to some degree the freedom on grazing land. Each cattle operation may vary slightly, depending upon the location of the home ranch, type of range, and time of year that feed is available at any given site. The overall pattern and routine remained fairly constant.

The following account dealing with these four cattlemen, who for over a quarter of a century ran cattle jointly on the Fish Creek Allotment, is given with the hope that it may furnish some insight into the great cattle industry and lives of families associated with it.

A cattleman's life is a series of predetermined annual events. Possibly breaking the yearly cycle in November, when the dry cattle (this means there are no cows with calves still nursing) are turned out on the winter range, is as good a place as any to begin.

The four Fish Creek cattlemen ran cow and calf outfits. This means that the cow herd was maintained year after year with only the bulk of the annual calf crop and old cows no longer producing calves, being sold. These were replaced by heifers from the calf crop so that the breeding herd was kept at the desired number.

Calves were usually born from the first of March through the month of May on the winter and spring range. At about eight months of age, they were weaned and kept on the ranch for three or four months. There they were fed hay and feed supplement, such as cottonseed cake. The calves were sold sometime after the first of the year when people became tired of eating turkey, and the beef market correspondingly improved. Always a certain number of cows with calves too small to wean were kept on the ranch and fed hay through the winter. The bulls were also kept on the ranch in the winter, and were not turned out with the cow herd until the latter part of June.

With this background, the cycle begins from when the calves have been taken from the cows and it is time to drive the dry cows to the winter range. The winter range is all government-owned land. Qualified cattlemen are issued grazing permits by the Bureau of Land Management. These permits entitle the holders to run a certain number of cattle over a predetermined area for a specified period of time.

Powers and Smith ranged most of their cattle on the Mojave Desert and in the canyons west of the desert, extending from Indian Wells Canyon to Little Lake Canyon, thirty miles to the north. The Alexander and Robertson herds wintered along Highway 178 from Onyx to Walker Pass and east of the pass as far as Freeman Junction.

At first glance, putting cattle out to graze on a desert may appear to be a futile endeavor. The dry, dead-looking brush seems incapable of making a good meal for a jackrabbit, much less a cow. Nevertheless, the cattle not only survive, but most years gain weight on their diet of brush, particularly salt brush, which has a great deal of food

David Perkins, Kern River Cowboy, and his horse Old Yeller.

value. One reason that these herds thrive on the desert in the winter is that they are composed primarily of the "dry" cattle . . . steers, yearlings and cows whose calves have been weaned. When first turned out, they still carry some of the fat accumulated during the summer, and their diet of brush is supplemented in the spring by flowering annuals.

When the time came to turn the cattle out on the winter range, Bill and Jim drove their herds together. The drive took about three days. On the way, some of the cattle were left scattered near waterholes along the route from Canebrake to Freeman Junction.

Stanley ran some of his cattle in the Canebrake country in winter and spring, and the rest were taken to the desert. On the first day of the drive, Stanley took his herd as far as Windmill Field, located a mile and a half below Walker Pass Lodge. On the second day, the cattle were driven over Walker Pass to Soldier Wells, a camp on the south side of Highway 178 and about three miles from Highway 14. The south end of Stanley's range was reached on the third day. A few head were dropped off in each of the canyons on the way to Little Lake. This final stage of the drive required one more day.

The route followed by Marvin Powers and his boys was much the same, except that they preferred to take a short-cut. They turned east in back of James' place, just below Walker Pass Lodge. Fol-

lowing this canyon, Three Pines Canyon, to the summit, they dropped over into Indian Wells Canyon on the desert side. On the desert, the herd was scattered in the canyons from the Homestead Cafe past Brady's Cafe on Highway 14. The desert canyons which supported Powers' and Smith's herds ranged from Indian Wells Canyon at the south, northward through Short Canyon, Grapevine, Sand Canyon, No Name, Nine Mile, Deadfoot, Five Mile, and finally, Little Lake Canyon.

Before the public domain was reclassified to testing ground by the U.S. Government, the area now occupied by the Naval Weapons Center at China Lake was also grazing land. There were few water holes and this part of the country was generally used only when the wild flowers were at their peak. The flowers contained abundant water in their stalks, enough to sustain the cattle for as long as two weeks without coming in for water.

Powers and Smith had a camp in Grapevine Canyon, just up the canyon past the aqueduct and on the north side of the creek. Here, a cowboy would batch in a small shack, with three or four horses and possibly a dog as his only company. His life was typical of line camp riders in any cattle country.

Every week or so he checked in at the main ranch to pick up groceries and mail. The rest of the time he was on his own. He rode a different part of the range every day, constantly checking the cattle on each section. When the cows started calving in March or April, he kept a close eye on any he had reason to believe might have a hard time.

The eyes of a cowboy are his best asset. As he rides, he can watch cattle in the distance and know whether or not everything is as it should be. If the cattle have stopped eating by ten or eleven o'clock in the morning and are lying in the shade of the Joshua trees, indications are that food is plentiful in that area.

An ability to interpret cattle tracks also helps the cowboy to ascertain the condition of his herd. A weak cow, one which perhaps has had trouble calving, leaves a distinctive set of tracks. Most cowboys can tell by looking at tracks how many cattle have moved across a certain area, how long ago, and the size and condition of the cattle.

In the movies, the horse ridden by the cowboy hero is depicted as a kind of equine Boy Scout . . . gentle, faithful, intelligent, helpful, kind, loving . . . a cowboy's best friend. So much for Hollywood. The truth is that many are just the opposite. Many a lone line rider has been seriously injured while riding young unbroken colts or horses with cantankerous dispositions. Some horses, like some people, are born mean. They will wait day after day just to catch a cowboy off guard. They will scheme for a chance to buck him off, kick him, or worse yet, buck him off and head back to camp, leaving the rider to hoof it across the desert. To a cowboy, this is the final humiliation. Most of them have no use whatever for walking, and will mount a horse to go a distance no greater than fifty feet.

There have been instances where a cowboy has been bucked off and lain injured for one or more days before being discovered by someone from the main ranch. Such incidents are accepted philosophically as part of the game; an occupational hazard. A cowboy would feel uneasy if he thought the bosses were too concerned about his physical well being. He has other things to worry about, and so do they.

From November through May, before the heat of the summer, the climate of the desert is ideal. Cold, crisp nights are followed by sunny days perfumed with the fragrance of sagebrush and, in spring, wild flowers. The occasional dust storms or, at times, snow flurries, only serve to keep a man on his toes.

Sometimes, more than one man was left at the Grapevine Camp. Such was the case with Clint Worlds, renowned cowboy artist, who camped with one of the Powers boys. One of Clint's favorite evening pastimes was to sketch the day's happenings—a wild bull roped or his partner getting bucked from a bronc—on pieces of cardboard box or anything handy while Powers gave his advice, which was really not needed. Clint also went to the high country for Smith and was a natural artist. His work was made so much better by completely knowing his field. Like most cowboys, he was a little eccentric at times.

He once startled Powers out of a sound sleep by shooting his 1934 Ford full of holes when it failed to start fast enough for an unscheduled trip to town. Another time, while at Fish Creek Camp, he attempted to show the boys how he could spur a bucking horse in the neck while perched on the hitching rack. He succeeded by getting both spurs caught on top of the rail in front of him and fell on his head in the dust.

Many of these incidents followed the sampling of "cough medicine." These events did not occur too often, and those who did use the hard stuff occasionally, did not let it interfere with their work.

In May, the Powers-Smith cattle started moving on their own toward Nine Mile Canyon. The crews came in and started working the range, driving everything ahead of them toward the summer pastures. Complicating the work of the cowboys were those cattle, and there were always a few, which did not care to be driven *anywhere*. They bunched up among the willows along the canyon bottom. In this dense, rattlesnake-infested brush, the men were obliged to dismount and work the cows through on foot.

As the Powers-Smith herd approached Chimney Meadow at the eastern edge of the Kern Plateau, they would begin to intermingle with the Alexander-Robertson cattle being worked up from Canebrake. Camp was set up at Chimney, occupied by about fifteen cowboys and cowgirls. Each shared the daily chores of camp life, from wrangling horses in the early morning to carrying water and cutting piñon pine for cooking. There were no roads into this country until 1930. All supplies and necessities were packed in on mules. Groceries packed into the high country were usually left in the kyacks, or pack boxes, which served as primitive cupboards.

From Chimney, the combined herd was driven on toward the South Fork of the Kern River. Some of the cows were so eager to reach the high country that they would abandon their calves. Some, of course, had to be driven every step of the way.

The beef—a big part of the meals for the men and women participating in the drive—was furnished by the permittees, the amount contributed being based upon the amount of cattle each man ran. For instance, Stanley Smith ran about 500 head, while Powers, Alexander, and Robertson, combined, had approximately 700 head. Therefore, as the butchering was done on a pro-rated basis, Stanley provided almost half of the beef.

Butchering usually took place in the evening. A fat heifer calf weighing about 500 pounds was driven into camp. One man would rope her by the head, holding the calf by taking turns of the rope around the saddle horn. Then, a second cowboy would come in and catch one or two hind feet in his loop. With the animal stretched out between the two ropes, another cowboy would tap her between the eyes with the back of a single-bit axe. The throat was cut immediately and the beef was bled quickly and completely.

The animal was then rolled on its back under a piñon tree, supported on either side by blocks to prevent it from rolling, and four men would begin skinning. A cut through the hide was made down the middle of the stomach from the head to the tail; the hide then would be slit from his initial cut up the inside of each leg. Normally, one man would work on each leg, skinning it out and cutting the foot off at the first joint, while leaving it attached to the hide. With the legs skinned out, they would progress down the sides to the back. The beef was rolled from side to side to facilitate removal of the hide. During removal, care was taken that the ears be left intact to assure there would be no question as to who had contributed the animal. After removal of the entrails, a gamble stick of oak, usually about two feet long, was inserted into holes cut above the hock of each hind leg. The gamble stick was then attached with a chain to a block and tackle and the beef raised to a convenient working level.

Almost none of the beef was wasted. In addition to the liver, heart, and sweetbreads, the marrow guts were considered a delicacy in cow camp. This is part of the intestine of a sucking calf which is filled with marrow-like substance. One calf may produce three or four feet of usable material. A knot is tied at each end to preserve the marrow, and the entire thing, along with the other edible entrails, were soaked overnight in salt water. It was then sliced into two-inch sections for cooking, rolled in seasoned flour, and fried crisp.

The beef was trimmed and, with all excess fat removed, was put into a large meat bag. It was then hung overnight and allowed to chill in the crisp mountain air. The next morning, it was cut into quarters, returned to the meat sack, and wrapped in bed rolls to protect it from the heat of the day. The process of hanging to chill each night and wrapping during the day was used in place of a refrigerator, and worked every bit as good. With many people in camp, it would be gone within ten days.

After all edibles had been removed from the entrails and the brain taken from the skull cavity, a cowboy would put a rope on the head and unusable entrails and drag them into the brush a quarter-mile from camp. There, they made a feast for coyotes, who could be heard from camp that night yelping and howling their appreciation for the meal.

Each day of the drive started early with the typical cow camp breakfast of bacon, eggs, biscuits or hot cakes, fried potatoes, pink beans and fresh beef liver, brains, and so forth. With such an early start, the work would generally be finished by three o'clock in the afternoon. There always seemed to be seven or eight children in camp. After the day's

ride, they amused themselves by practicing their roping, or looking for Indian arrowheads and other artifacts.

The older children could usually coax or bully one of the smaller fry to take the part of the calf in the roping practice. The little one would run while the others would attempt to rope his feet. The ropers never tired of the game, but a halt was called when the make-believe calf ran out of steam, or was jerked down hard once too often.

It is rare that four families could work and live so closely for so many years without major differences arising. Life at camps such as Chimney Meadows and the South Fork of the Kern River prove that it can be done. It may have been a good combination of personalities.

The little cabin at Chimney Meadows measured about ten by twenty feet. Lumber for this cabin was packed in on mules over two feet of snow during March of 1920. Mort S. Hall precut and packaged the cabin at the ranch. It was hauled to the foot of the hill by wagon, then packed on the mules to Chimney. The cabin was of single-wall construction of one inch by twelve inch boards on a two inch by four inch frame. There was no insulation, and the floor of one-by-twelves was covered with black roofing paper. In later years, it was sealed, insulated, and had a new floor installed. But in the old days, it turned mighty cold inside when the wind whistled up the canyon and the fog hung low.

At one end of the cabin was a large wood-burning cookstove. Along one side, below two double windows, was an eight foot long table, flanked by benches. A smaller table near the stove, and a double bed in the corner, completed the furnishings. The bed was usually allotted to one of the older couples. Everyone else slept out under the stars.

In the 1940's, a small barn in which to store hay was built of corrugated sheet metal below the house. This caused Stanley to say to Marvin, "Did I tell you I built a barn at Chimney?" Marvin, who was always a great kidder, replied, "You had a barn, why didn't you build a house?"

Although rattlesnakes were encountered almost every day on the desert, they were a special hazard at the camps at Chimney and the South Fork. Every time someone came into camp, he had to walk rather cautiously until he had checked it out for snakes. You can bet the beds were checked before climbing in at night, too.

Almost everyone had a bedroll . . . the forerunner of the sleeping bag. Components of the bedroll were a piece of heavy canvas about sixteen feet long and eight feet wide, a mattress two or three inches thick, blankets, quilts, sheet blankets, and a pillow. Some beds had so many quilts a man could barely throw it on top of the pack.

The canvas was spread on the ground, then the mattress was placed on the upper part so that the remainder of the canvas could be folded over toward the center, and the snaps that were affixed to the outside edges were fastened together in the center. For transportation or storage, the centers were snapped, the bedroll rolled tightly, and then neatly tied with a small rope.

Cowboys always took their clothes to bed under the canvas to keep them free of the morning dew. Damp Levis at daybreak are a shock to the system. Those who retired before dark or arose after daylight soon became quite adept at dressing and undressing under the canvas, as there were no dressing rooms. It has been said that humans dress up, and cowboys dress down. The hat would go on first; next the shirt, if taken off—which most were not. A Levi jacket would follow, to guard against morning chill. Pants were pulled on, then socks. Boots were the only item of dress to be put on after the canvas was thrown back.

As the last of the herd approached the South Fork, camp was moved from Chimney Meadows to the river. Before the Nine Mile Road was built in 1930, this move entailed transporting all necessary gear fifteen miles on mules. After that time, trucks were used.

The river camp was much less luxurious than that at Chimney. It consisted entirely of a wood stove on a small, sandy beach above the Kern. When the drive to the mountains was on, usually toward the last of June, the weather was mild enough to make camping in the open quite enjoyable. Bringing the cattle out in the fall, with snow flying, was something else again.

Two small cabins have since been built at the river camp, the first of which burned down. They were nothing elaborate, but simply shelter from weather and a place to cook and eat. The South Fork folks have been a hardy breed, and most prefer sleeping in the open, rather than under a roof.

The loose horses were driven to the river from Chimney. There were usually more than forty head, all eager to be on the move. It was all that one man could do to hold them to a lope or even a fast trot. It never took long to cover the distance between camps.

Once at the river, the horses were turned into a 100 acre field. A wrangler horse remained in a smaller field close to camp. Each morning, shortly after daylight, one of the children would ride out and run the horses back into a corral near the camp. The kids took turns at this detail. Many a wild ride was taken over the sagebrush as the young rider ran the wrangling horse full tilt in an effort to turn the willful horses who had decided against confinement.

During the four or five days camp was set up at the river, cattle continued to be brought up from the winter range. The South Fork of the Kern River forms the boundary between lands under the jurisdiction of the Bureau of Land Management and those of the Forest Service.

The cattle are worked to arrive at the river on a date set by the Forest Service, at which time they may be counted onto the high country summer range. Counting through the drift fence usually begins around July first. A drift fence was designed, as the name implies, to prevent cattle from drifting onto a range where they did not belong or off a range where they did.

In the 1940's, a man by the name of Calahan took over the old Chet Smith homestead down Big Pine Creek. This site later became known as the Old Baldy Scout Ranch. Calahan had a primitive sort of night club there and, as it was only a twenty minute drive from the river camp, some of the young cowboys occasionally would jump in a pickup to go take a look at the bright lights. It was a popular spot for many from the big city.

One who spent quite a bit of time at Calahans was Stuart Hamblin. He had a pack of hounds and used to hunt bear and lion while staying there. On one of his hunting trips to this area, he stumbled onto the homesteader's cabin, which prompted him to write the song, "This Old House."

Cattle were counted at two locations, both of which were established around 1910. One was southwest of the river bridge, and the other above Kennedy Meadow Campground. While the physical sites have remained the same, the coming of roads has had a pronounced effect on the original character of this land.

The cattle were bunched near the gate through which they were to pass. As the animals crowded through a few at a time, a cattleman—usually Stanley—stood on the left of the gate, calling out the brand of each animal. A Forest Ranger noted each brand on a tally sheet as it was called. Each cattleman was allowed to graze a certain number of cattle as specified in his permit. For this number, the Forest Service charged so many cents per head per month. Only the grown cattle were counted. Calves under six months of age were given a free ride on National Forest pasturage.

The animals counted through at Kennedy Campground headed up-river into the country south of Monache Meadows. Those which passed through the southern gate worked their way up toward Rodeo Flat and into the area north of Fish Creek and Troy Meadow Campground.

The range used by the four Fish Creek permittees encompassed thirty square miles—or 90,000 acres—much of it being too mountainous and rocky for cattle. These cattlemen and their families knew most of these acres intimately. The areas that they did not enter during their summer cattle work, they covered while deer hunting or fishing, and the people loved each mountain meadow and timbered slope. The four permittees, being God-fearing men, and with the realization that they were only leasing this portion of the forest, felt as though they were entrusted with the safe-keeping of this vast acreage by God.

The boundaries of the summer range were Monache Meadows and the Monache drift fence on the north; Beach Ridge on the west, where the ridge acted as a natural barrier; and Bald Mountain to the south, again unfenced, the border being Bald Mountain Saddle. Usually only about 1,200 head of grown stock were run on the combined permits.

Four summer camps were used by the cattlemen and their families. Bill Alexander's was at Powell Meadow; Marvin Powers' at Granite Knob; and the Smith's and Robertson's on upper Fish Creek, all about a mile apart.

Everyone concerned looked forward throughout the winter and spring to the day when it would be time for the outfits to move into the high country. As many as twenty adults and children would make up the party. Age was no barrier. Babies rode on pillows in front of their parents, or were comfortably settled in well padded kyacks, firmly secured to a mule. At least ten pack mules or horses completed the entourage. Pack animals carrying quantities of bedding and other light, bulky objects seemed to all but disappear under the load, looking more like a huge bedroll with legs, ears, and tail.

Though cattlemen were expert packers, packing time was always hectic, at best. Having been idle for five or six months, there was ample time for some mules to work up a distinct aversion to carrying anything other than their own natural hides.

Snow and freezing weather wreaked havoc with fences. The first job on arrival in the high country was to repair the fence on the wrangling pasture. This was a small pasture, usually about half an acre, in which a horse could be caught quickly and used to run in the other horses. After the wrangling pasture was secured, the other fences were tended to.

The summer camps were at an elevation of approximately 8,000 feet. The nights were cold and the days were glorious. When the cattle first came into the mountains in the spring, the snow was almost entirely melted, with just a patch or two remaining in heavily timbered areas. The growing season was short at this elevation, but it seemed that Mother Nature made allowances for this by accelerating the cycle to the point where one could almost see the grass and flowers grow. A hundred varieties of flowers bloomed in the mountain meadows, their fragrance mingling with the spicy scent of the pines.

The fishing done by the younger generation at the South Fork camp was insignificant when compared with the thrill of catching the wary golden trout of the high country. The streams were small, and in some spots, almost overgrown. Most originated from springs some distance on up the mountain. The fish were small, being normally only six to eight inches—just frying pan size. They were usually hungry, too. One fish per cast was almost a guarantee.

All the horses were kept at Stanley Smith's field until the other men could repair their fences, then they were moved to the individual pastures. The men lucky enough to go early with the horses would quickly patch up the fence around the horse pasture, or wrangling field, then grab a fishing pole and head for the creek. It was considered an honor to bring in the first limit of trout for the year. Soon, the rest of the outfit arrived and moved on to their individual camps. By sundown, there would be fish in each camp. The aroma of trout fried in bacon grease would drift from each cooking fire the next morning.

The ranchers pooled their manpower in order to get their fences repaired as quickly as possible. This usually took four or five days, giving the cattle time to reach the meadows and rest up for the spring branding. Branding time was the highlight of the year for most of those involved, and particularly for the younger folks. Many of the kids would

Pioneer Kern County Cattlemen in 1965. From left: Jim Robertson, Walker Rankin, Jr. and Stanley Smith.

rather rope than eat, and never seemed to get enough of it during the rest of the year. Branding corrals were set up at various locations on the range so the scattered cattle would not have to be driven any great distance.

Seven o'clock in the morning found all hands assembled at Stanley Smith's camp. Stanley, the rodeo boss, would then inform them of the plans for the day. If the branding was to take place at Beck Meadows, for instance, Stanley might have said something like this:

> Bill and Leonard, go through Corral Meadows and work the country around Little Bull Meadows. Come out at the head of Beck and meet us at the rodeo ground. Marvin, you take your boys and work Lost Meadow, pushing them down Lost Creek to Beck. Jim, you and your family work the country around Swallow Point and along the drift fence. I'll take my outfit and ride through the Inyo County cattle on the other side of Monache drift fence. We'll pick up any of the cattle that might have gotten through the fence.

Usually the instructions were not even as lengthy as this. Everyone knew what was expected when riding a certain part of the country. Any of the others could have made these decisions, but Stanley had been chosen and he did a good job.

The work generally followed the same pattern, year after year. Seven days were needed to complete the branding, one day being spent at each of the following meadows: Albanita, Broder, Beck, Smith, Jackass, and Troy. Each location had its branding corral, built of logs. The seventh day was pick-up day, when everyone would scatter over the range and drive any unbranded calves and their mothers back to Fish Creek. They would be branded at Smith Meadow and turned loose.

Each rider or group of riders would complete his circle by ten o'clock and begin arriving at the rodeo ground. When all riders were accounted for, one of the permittees would begin to cut out his cows and calves. The cattle were maintained in a loose bunch as the cattlemen cut out their cows and unmarked calves. Each moved his stock in a different direction away from the main herd, and kept them separate to await their turn in the branding corral. Cutting from the herd was over by noon, and the branding fire was started.

A mule, loaded with brands, medicine, and lunch, was usually led out to the branding site. This was one of the few times when the cattlemen ate lunch when out riding. A coffee pot on the branding fire would produce the brew to accompany anything from bean sandwiches to cold trout or steak, cold biscuits, canned tomatoes or peaches, and big squares of Hershey's chocolate.

Then branding began. The smallest group of calves was taken to the branding corral first in order to free the men holding them. As soon as their cut, or bunch, was branded and turned loose, they helped with the others.

There was something intriguing about calf branding that was hard to explain. In a setting of pine-fringed meadows and crystal clear sky, a calf was marked with its owner's brand; a puff of pungent smoke, and the calf ran bawling to its mother. Each phase of the operation combined to create a scene that was eagerly anticipated, even by old-timers who had taken part in the annual event all their lives.

Two to four men worked in the corral on horseback, roping the calves. When two men worked together, the one who caught the last calf by the hind feet would give his partner the first throw at the next calf. If he missed his first throw, either man was free to try. Some of the top ropers have roped for hours at a time and never missed catching both hind feet with every loop that left their hand. However, it was observed that no matter how fast a man could get another loop built, or how good a roper his partner was, he would give the other man first shot at the hind feet if he had caught the last one. This was part of the unwritten code of the West.

Bill Alexander roping calves in the corral at Smith's camp. The cowboy putting the brand on is unidentified.

As one man caught the calf by the hind feet and dragged it to the fire, the second man roped the animal by the head. If the calf was very small, the second rope was not used until reaching the fire, at which time the calf would be flanked, or thrown. A rope was put on its front feet and the animal stretched out. That is, each horse maintained enough tension on the rope to prevent the calf from kicking loose.

Lois Alexander Vig roping calves in the high country in the 1940's.

Keith Alexander with his son, Kit.

In working cattle, the horse was all-important. Whether in or out of the corral, a good roping horse put a rider in the best position to make his throw and kept the rope taut at all times after the catch had been made. A good cow horse did many small but important details on his own. It was a joy to ride such a good horse or to watch him perform. A good roper became infinitely better on a horse with enough savvy to give his rider every advantage.

The branding fire was located inside the gate of the larger corrals and outside the smaller ones. When a calf reached the fire, a crew of four or five men, women, and kids went to work. Most difficult of the chores was to flank the calf, or tail it down. A great deal of teamwork was required to get a big, ten-month-old calf to the ground. If the heeler caught both hind feet, the header would put his loop on the head, and the calf would be pulled to the ground by the tail. But, if only one foot was caught, a rope was many times put on the head, too. One man would grab the rope to the hind foot on the opposite side to which he was standing, another cowboy would then grab the calf's tail, and as they gave a pull together, the animal's free leg was jerked out from under it.

The ropers would let a little slack in the rope. The calf was jerked down. The man who had the tail jumped to the shoulder of the calf and pulled its front foot back and upward, bracing his knees against the calf's neck and shoulders. The other flanker pulled the calf's tail between its legs and, maintaining a steady pull, reached forward with one hand to remove the rope from the hind foot. Crossing the hind feet, he put the loop back on and then held it tight until the roper had taken his turns on the saddle horn with his rope—or "dallied," as it is called—and backed his horse. The man who held the front foot took the rope off the head, crossed the front feet, slipped the loop around them, and the calf was ready to work on.

Registered brands are generally placed on the left side of the animal, so the calf is stretched out on its right side. Each family usually handled the branding and earmarking of its own calves. By the time a child was twelve or thirteen years old, he could do all of the tasks involved in branding, and do them well.

First shot at the grounded calf went to the man who did the earmarking and castrating. It takes about one minute to castrate à bull calf. The by-products of the procedure, called "mountain oysters," were collected by one of the kids. They were then cooked on the coals at the edge of the branding fire and eaten on the spot. A roper who had a spare minute would ride over to get his share. They were consumed, as is, unwashed, unsalted, and unseasoned. The taste is similar to frog legs or chicken.

The earmark is a great deal more important than the brand, as it can be seen and recognized at a distance of up to a quarter of a mile. In the winter, when the hair on the hide is fairly long, a brand is relatively difficult to read. But a well made earmark is easily discernible.

Each cattleman has his earmark made in a particular way, and those who perform the operation make certain to mark it just that way. Marvin Powers used an earmark like this ⊂ ⊃ . His brand was a circle dot ⊙ on the left hip. Stanley Smith used ⊂ ⊃ and the |3 brand on the left hip. Jim Robertson used ⊂ ⊃ with the bar wrench brand ⩑ on the left hip. This brand was patterned after the old wagon wrench used to remove the wheel nuts. Bill Alexander's earmark was a ⊂ ⊃ . His brand, ⅂ℓ, called the Seven H. L., was placed on the left ribs.

While the marker worked on the head, the calf was vaccinated against Black Leg Fever and branded. Each brand was usually placed correctly, but occasionally one of the kids would slip and the brand was positioned too high or too low. Whoever misplaced the brand would be reminded of it every time that particular animal showed up on the range. As the brand was put on with a rocking motion, the smoke turned from brown to blue. This indicated that the hair was burned through, hide had been reached, and a good brand achieved.

Stanley Smith always dehorned his calves as he earmarked. He felt that they were easier to feed in winter and would bring a little more at market without horns. The others claimed that the cows could more readily keep the coyotes away from small calves if allowed to keep their horns. Pine tar was applied to the open cut on the bull calves, and to the head if the calf had been dehorned. This was done to keep flies away. In years when the screw worms were bad, even the earmark was dabbed, and the calves had to be watched closely all summer. Many times they had to be roped and doctored out on the range if they showed signs of having worms. A calf seen shaking his head or wringing his tail was most likely needing attention. This is where experience was most valuable, as a cowhand could usually tell the condition of cattle simply by observing them as he rode past.

Branding proceeded at a fast clip and, although nobody seemed to be rushing, there was no lost motion as, on most branding days, there was a long ride back to camp afterwards. At Beck Meadows, this involved about a ten-mile ride. The youngsters used to slip off in the lead and race down through the timbered slopes, jumping logs and dodging limbs. This was not a very safe sport, and not the best thing in the world for the horses, some of which were spoiled in this way. They became so inclined that they would always want to run to camp. No one was ever seriously injured, though. A little hide taken off was considered to be part of the game.

A good horse under a cowboy makes a good cowhand even better. Every cattleman had his favorite horses that he owned during his lifetime. Bill Aleck's favorites were Buck, Johnny, and Sleepy. Jim swore by Butch and Baldy. With Marvin, it was Frenchy, Cowboy, and Cedar. Stanley's many favorites included Pedro, Frank, Joker, Sheif, Smokey, Napoleon, and Chico. These horses never won prizes at the County Fair, but many of them could have. They were top working horses, which could carry a man all day.

Sometimes on the fall trips, one horse would be ridden every day for a week. This really showed how much stamina a horse had. Those horses that did win ribbons were good at one thing. The working cow horses, however, never specialized, but most were equally skilled at roping, cutting, and carrying the cowboy at any speed through rough country as he made his daily ride. The South Fork cattlemen were blessed with many fine riders who worked with them over the years. It would be impossible to name all of them, but a few outstanding men come to mind. Brock Cole worked for all of the cattlemen at one time or another. Brock had a lot of tall tales to tell. He had the gift of gab and kept up a constant chatter. He was well liked by all as there was never a dull moment when he was around. Tough as a hickory nut, Brock would make the fall trip into the mountains wearing a light shirt and old jumper. Most of the others would have long underwear, chaps and heavy coats, yet still seem to feel the cold more than Brock. Brock was always getting off his horse and setting a sagebrush afire, which was the only thing that indicated he might be cold.

Freddy Burke and Alphonso Redarte rode for Jim Robertson for many years, as did William Petersen for Bill Alexander. Another old-timer, an Arizona cowboy named Harvey Robinson, rode herd on the Alexander-Robertson cattle while on the winter and summer range. Jimmy and Johnny Chico often helped Marvin Powers with the cattle, as did Art Cole and Hoot McDonald. Stanley Smith had the biggest bunch of cattle, and so he hired more outside help, many of whom worked

Rockhouse Meadow Cow Camp. Stanley Smith (left) with Celso Vega. Celso was one of the best cowboys to ever ride the Fish Creek Range.

year around for Smith. These men were not only top hands when it came to working the cattle and horses, but also were welcome additions in the cow camps, where they helped on everything from washing dishes to cutting wood. Among those who will be longest remembered were Paul Rhoads, Smiley Ramos, Red Vega, Willie Andreas, Tony Pablo, and Walt Mecham. Others who worked for shorter periods for Smith were Buster Rhoads, Ray Milligan, Sid Andreas, and Lyman Peterson.

After the branding had been finished at all locations, everyone would take a few days off in camp. This gave time to check over clothing that needed washing. Most of the cattle people dressed about the same. Levis were usually worn, along with blue cotton workshirts. Long handled underwear was substituted for the conventional type, much of the time, for extra warmth. Unlined Levi jackets were popular and, when not being worn, were tied behind the saddle. The cowman's hat had as much personality as the man himself, and was discarded only when completely worn out. Everyone who rode on the Fish Creek range remembers how Bill Aleck put his hat on and then pulled it down and around as if he were screwing it on, so that the front always faced a little to the side.

More money was put into boots than any other

Paul Rhoads at the Old Palmer Ranch in the 1930's.

Red Vega and Smiley Ramos on the Smith Ranch.

item of clothing. Most of the riders ordered through Western or Bloocher Boot Companies, where their measurements were kept on record. Some of the men wore a small silk scarf around their neck. When water had to be carried from the creek, heated on a wood stove, and clothes hand scrubbed, shirts were not changed every time a bit of mud got on them. The Levi pants seldom got as much washing as other articles of clothing. Some of the younger cowboys actually preferred to wear them without washing until they were almost completely worn out. They could step out of them, and the pants would stand up themselves. As long as they didn't try to walk off by themselves, they were not considered too dirty. Although seldom washed, they were "dry cleaned" almost daily. This consisted of scraping off everything, including corral dirt, with one's pocket knife. More than one young bride found herself in hot water by deciding her cowboy husband needed to have all his Levis washed.

The time spent in camp was also used to care for any horses needing shoeing, although this was done many times when the men came back to camp early from a regular day's ride. The horses had to be re-shod every six weeks or so, and each rancher took care of his own horses. Most had learned to shoe horses as boys watching their dads. Often, there would be some genuine excitement around camp when a colt or one of the broke horses was being shod and did not quite like the idea. None were too tough to handle, and, although gentleness was the rule, it was considered okay to attract their attention by whacking them along the ribs with a shoeing rasp. A hind foot might have to be tied up or an animal thrown to the ground to get shoes on him, but this was the exception. If the horse was started right, he usually accepted the shoeing process as part of the routine.

A few days off were also used to wash saddle blankets and make repairs on their riding gear. Great care was taken with the horse's back. Saddles were not only bought to fit well, but clean saddle blankets were a must. Many cattlemen used a two-fold wool blanket next to the horse's back—turned and refolded as it got dirty. Two sets of blankets were generally on hand so that one could be washed while the other was in use. Prior to being saddled, the animals always received a good brushing on the back and other parts covered by the saddle. On a long, hot pull, the men would get off and, after loosening the cinch, prop the back of their saddle up by resting an elbow on the horse's back. This allowed a little air onto the mount's back.

Although many types of bits were used, many of the riders favored the Spanish, or spade, bit. Most popular were those made by Abie Hunt, a pioneer Kern County bit maker. These bits may look inhumane, but if made and used right, a horse gets used to the feel of one in his mouth and can be kept with a "light mouth" all his life.

Split leather reins were used to a good degree, but some leaned toward the use of braided rawhide or leather reins, with romel attached. Rawhide reatas were carried by most of the old-timers in lieu of the newer grass or nylon ropes. But as it became harder to get good rawhide work done, they gradually switched over. Jim Robertson, the last old-timer to pack a rawhide reata on the Fish Creek range, used this type of rope until his retirement. Willie Nicoll was remembered as being an artist with a reata. Carrying a 50-footer, he would swing an eight-foot loop and reach out for an unbelievably long distance, seldom missing.

Some of the hands occasionally broke down and took a bath. One such event that took place at Smith's camp will be long remembered. The men were butchering beef. After letting the men know in which direction they were headed, a couple of young school teachers and some of the other young ladies headed up the creek. A quarter mile up, and well out of sight, was a good, sandy pool, about knee deep and five or six feet across. On one side was a big flat rock on which to dry off.

This was in the 1930's and the pool was twenty miles from the nearest road, so there was not a chance in a thousand that anyone would ride up on them. There simply was nobody except cattlemen in that part of the country. No bathing suits were packed into the mountains, yet they felt as safe as if at the Y.W.C.A. They had taken their baths and were sunning themselves on the rock. Back at camp, someone got a bright idea; one of the women in the camp would ride up the creek and give the girls a scare. Gwen Smith, always a good sport, volunteered to do the honors. The girls knew that the entrails of the butchered animal would be dragged out that way, but figured the men would wait until they were back in camp.

Riding Red Vega's horse, Buddy, and wearing Red's hat and jumper, Gwen broke though the

A.B. (Abie) Hunt, pioneer bit maker of Kern County.

small trees near the swimming hole, head down, and dragging the entrails. The ladies were laughing and talking and thereby did not see Gwen until she was fifty or sixty feet away. When spotted, from what Mrs. Smith says, it was really a sight to see those girls all try to hide in that little shallow pool.

A lot of good-natured kidding went on around the camps. This included anything from finding your bed in the top of a pine tree to having a coiled rope placed under your bed and pulled out slowly just as you were going to sleep. Although rattlesnakes were not too common at this elevation, they were quite thick in the lower country. The sensation of having a snake in bed with you caused many a rapid change of location. Generally, these people were a happy bunch, doing what they enjoyed, and working as a family group.

With branding finished, and everyone rested up, the group headed back to the valley to put up the second cutting of hay. One man stayed behind to watch the cattle. Almost everyone hated to leave, but there was very little time in this cattle operation to spend loafing in the high country. The worst part was having to ride back down into the heat of the South Fork after three or four weeks of ideal daytime temperature.

After about three weeks in the valley, the work

Earl Phillips and unknown victim getting a haircut at the Smith Cabin, Fish Creek. Once Earl broke his collarbone while camped at this cabin. A doctor rode in 50 miles to set the broken bone, and Earl stayed in the mountains until it healed. This cabin, built in 1900, was still being used by the Smith family in 1987.

in the hayfields was finished. The families headed back to the high country. Most of them took guests along. Many of these guests cherished the memories of beef gathering at Fish Creek.

Each of the cattlemen, with the exception of Stanley Smith, used a gathering field furnished by the Forest Service. Stanley owned his own meadow at Fish Creek. By coming up Fish Creek, the first camp along the way was Jim Robertson's. Jim built a comfortable cabin about 10 by 18 feet, with a cook shed in front, for Ann and himself. Except in the fall, not too much time was spent in the cabin when the hands were there. Usually everyone sat around the cooking area. There was a good wood cookstove, both under the cook shed and inside the cabin. Most of the kitchen utensils were hung on nails from the cabin wall or on the wall at the back of the shed.

These mountaineers could put out a good meal with a cast iron frying pan, one kettle, a Dutch oven, and a coffee pot . . . and they put it out in a hurry. Anyone who has ever camped at Robertson's remembers Jim's Dutch oven biscuits. Dutch oven

cooking is an art that has all but disappeared, and Jim was a master at it. The Dutch oven is a cast iron kettle, ten inches to twenty-four inches across. A rim around the lid held the coals. Some had short legs, though these were not necessary. There were two types of cooking done in a Dutch oven. By burying the oven in a pit and leaving it for four or five hours, you could cook a batch of beans, roast, or stew, or anything that required a long time. By the other method, you baked in the open. Such things as biscuits and pies baked in this fashion were hard to beat.

For biscuits, a fire was built ahead of time. As the fire burned down to coals, the oven and lid were preheated. The inside of the oven was treated in a very special way. Old-time cooks never washed the inside in order to preserve the interior conditioning, or seasoning, as it was called. If it ever became necessary to wash the oven, the interior was reconditioned by heating the oven and rubbing a raw potato into the pores of the metal. A wooden hook was used to place the oven where you wanted it. The oven was carried by hooking the metal bail, and the lid was carried by the small handle on top.

Stanley Smith's cabin was small, about eight by sixteen feet. It was built by an old-timer named Ed Pettypool in 1900. In 1928, the year Stanley and Gwen were married, a sign was hung over the door: "You have had your wedding bells. From now on it's cow bells and tin cans." It hung over the door for forty years, and finally the weather finished it.

Sitting at the twelve foot tables in the cook shed, you could look down across the 100-acre meadow. In the evening, sometimes as many as twenty deer would cautiously enter the meadow. Groundhogs napped in the sun around Ground Hog Point, a pile of rocks that stuck out into the meadow, or early in the morning you could watch one of the kids running the horses across the frosty meadow as they worked their way through the sagebrush and into the pines to the corral.

This was always done at a dead run. If the horses were brought in slowly, they would try to break back. The wrangle horse was usually ridden bareback. The kids could ride like little Indians, their horses dodging trees and jumping logs, sagebrush and creeks.

A large range, or cookstove, stood at the north end of the cook shed. It was quite a job to get it up to the camp. Even after it was stripped of all removable parts, it weighed 400 pounds, and had to be packed in on a mule the last eighteen miles.

Gwen Smith in the 1930's. Gwen was the first wife of the Fish Creek permittees to go to the mountains with her husband to camp and work cattle.

Gary Alexander, raised in the Kern River Valley, graduated from Fresno State College in January 1968 with a B.S. in Animal Husbandry. He worked for Henry Levy of Merced, California for 14 years. In 1987 Levy and Alexander were partners on leased ranches around Merced.

A big gray mule named Dick did the honors. Although he tried to buck it off before it was tied down, he went all the way with the stove. This was the heaviest load ever packed into the back country by an animal. Dick's fame did not last long, however. The following year, he was bitten in the face by a rattlesnake as he reached for a mouthful of grass, and he died from the bite. The big range had a grill on each side. Tons of beef steaks cooked on them were without equal, even in restaurants where the cost of a good steak was exorbitant.

There was always a big, black, two-gallon coffee pot at the back of the stove. As the fire almost never went out during the waking hours, you could get a cup of hot coffee anytime. A little more water and a little more coffee were added until the grounds built up too far. At that point, they were thrown out, the pot rinsed, and coffee making started again. This coffee had real body to it and could not be duplicated by any of the modern methods.

Wood for cooking was never a problem. Some of the crew would go out on the hill above camp and fell a dead lodgepole pine, occasionally referred to as a "tamarack," about thirty inches through, with a two-man handsaw called a "misery whip."

The limbs that did not break when it fell were chopped off and hauled into camp on a homemade sled called a stone boat, pulled by one of the pack

mules. These limbs, called "squaw wood," were two to five inches in diameter and made an excellent cooking fire. It could be broken easily into desired lengths by popping it over a log. Keeping the wood box filled was a chore that usually belonged to the youngsters. They also were in charge of carrying water from the spring, wrangling the horses, and milking the cow if there happened to be one in camp.

At the Powers' camp, cooking was done in the open until the 1930's. Then Marvin had his boys put up a small, sheet metal cabin. The main attraction of this cabin was a Home Comfort cook stove. The biscuits and golden trout for breakfast, or haunch of venison cooked in the oven, to accompany the ever-present pot of beans simmering at the back of the stove, could never be forgotten by those who camped there.

Within 100 yards of the Powers' camp were many trees that had been blown down by heavy winter winds. It was never necessary to cut down a tree or to walk very far for firewood at this camp. A spring bubbled up from white sands fifty yards from camp. A trough was so designed and built that a bucket placed under the trough was soon filled with the coldest, clearest water ever tasted. It

Johnny Potter, a Kern River cowboy.

was so cold that you had to sip it to avoid setting your teeth on edge.

The Powers' cabin was located at the east edge of Granite Knob Meadow so as to catch the first rays of the sun filtering through the pines on the chilly summer mornings. The rising sun chased the frost from the meadow, exposing a profusion of wild flowers among the lush grasses.

Tents were provided for those who did not care to sleep in the open. There was never much chance for anyone to oversleep. Just about the time the sun peeked around Jackass Peak, the squirrels and chipmunks began a self-appointed job of waking everyone in camp. They dropped small pine cones on the tents and ran full tilt up and down the tent's ridgepole, chattering all the while. They were forgiven at meal times, though, when they would scurry across the dirt floor of the cabin and perch themselves close by to beg for tidbits from the table.

As the first star appeared in the evening, a campfire was built. Not many people stayed up later than nine o'clock because of early rising the next day. Nevertheless, these evenings spent around the fire, with possibly some accordion music by Bill Powers, or a few tunes on the harmonica by Marvin, Jr., were more pleasant, by far, than any spent in overstuffed chairs in front of a television set. A

poem by Jud Jordan, who spent many a night in this high country, ably conveys the feelings one can hold about this experience.

FISH CREEK CAMP

I've lain in my blankets at nightime
With the star studded heavens o'er head;
With my camp trappings scattered about me
And the dying campfire glowing red.
And it seemed that the God who created
These wonders so long, long ago,
Came close to me there in the silence
And spoke to me things I should know.
The sage-scented breezes of evening
Came whispering up from the plain,
And the dew, falling soft on the meadow,
Brought with it the freshness of rain.
The moon riding high in the heavens,
Bathed the peaks in a mantle of light,
While the tree studded canyons below them
Lay dark in the stillness of night.
The creek flowing down through the meadow
Sang a song to night's arches of blue,
And it shone like a ribbon of silver
Where the pines let the moonbeams drift through.
The quavering cry of a coyote
Came faint on the murmuring breeze,
And my eyelids grew heavy with slumber
To the whispered good-night of the trees.

J. H. Jordan
Bakersfield, California

Don Powers in the high country in the 1930's.

84

Bill Alexander's camp and holding field was located at Powell Meadow, about a mile north of Smith's. Bill and his family required even less in the way of modern conveniences. The only permanent fixtures in their camp were a large homemade stove and table. Built up with rock and cement, the stove had a large cast iron top with three lengths of stove pipe attached to it. It would take logs up to eight inches in diameter and thirty inches long, and would keep a pot of beans or stew cooking most of the day if you filled it in the morning. The lodgepole pine table was about ten feet long, with benches attached, and covered with linoleum. Everything else used in the camp was either stored at Stanley's or packed out each winter.

Try to picture, if you will, sitting down at camp to a good steak or mess of golden trout with Dutch oven biscuits and all the trimmings, while all about was the cool shade of the pines and firs and clean, crisp air. For entertainment, there might be a couple of fawns romping on the far side of the meadow, or a coyote out to catch a meal of grasshoppers or gophers, as well as chipmunks scurrying through camp. The saucy bluejays and camp robbers were always around at meal times, their cries and the distant drumming of woodpeckers blending with the murmuring of the mountain stream. Such a setting made good food even better. Many times, bears would come into camp at night. They managed to carry off quite a bit of food, and at one time, got away with a whole hind quarter of beef.

None of these camps were fancy. But to the families who each summer migrated to the High Sierra with their cattle, it was a second home.

The agreement these cattlemen had with the Forest Service required them to bring part of their herds out of the mountains toward the last of August. The exact date varied, being governed by how well the feed was holding up.

The first gathering was handled as with branding. Each day, cattle from a certain part of the range were worked to a central location. Here, each permittee cut out forty percent of his cattle to take to the home ranch. Beef cattle were generally selected, as, by this time, they were in prime condition. These were taken to the holding pastures at each camp, where they put on a few extra pounds. The meadows were still high with feed, having supported only a few head of saddle horses during the summer.

After the range was completely worked, they began what they called the beef cattle drive. Each family drove its own stock, and usually followed a day behind another drive. The fifty miles to the valley was covered in about four days, with the families camping along the way.

Care was taken to handle the cattle in a manner which would keep the pounds on them, with very little of the running and jostling depicted in movies. The mark of a good cowboy was his ability to ride hard and fast when the need arose. But to be content to poke along with the cattle while traveling, letting them more or less pick their own speed and keeping them from losing any more weight than was absolutely necessary, this also was quite important, as those pounds meant dollars.

Usually Art Alexander at the Onyx Ranch, or his partner, Oscar Rudnick, of Bakersfield, bought the cattle. In the early days, cattlemen would deliver the beef cattle to the slaughter house in Bakersfield, which involved an extra 75-mile drive by way of Caliente.

While the cattlemen were in the valley after this trip, the third cutting of hay was usually put up, provided the river persisted long enough to furnish water for this last crop.

If any part of the year was to be a vacation, it was after the return to the mountains for the last trip. This was usually early in the first part of deer season. The cattlemen had learned years ago that you could not get much work out of a South Fork cowboy until he had a chance to get some of the buck hunting out of his system. Just about everyone hunted, and cattlemen like Marvin and Stanley were the first to understand, because if either one of them had a hobby, it was deer hunting. They came by it honestly, since their fathers before them had looked forward to this time of year. So the men usually were given about three days to hunt, with pay. Within a day or two, quite a few bucks were hanging in the shade around the camps. Deer heart and liver would be sizzling in the breakfast pan each morning.

At this time, the youngsters were usually in school, and the wives stayed on the ranch. During this last trip, the weather was getting pretty cold, and crawling out into the frosty morning appealed more to the men than to the women, although the latter could endure it if the occasion arose. Not enough can be said about these ranchers' wives— Gwen Smith, Dorothy Alexander, Isabell Powers, and Ann Robertson. All of them rode with the men most of the year and still had time to raise families and do most of the cooking, to say nothing of washing clothes with scrub board and old-time clothes squasher in a washtub heated on a wood fire. Even keeping the children halfway clean was difficult in the mountains where, when they were not riding, the young ones would be sliding down the banks along the creeks or sloshing through the muddy areas of the meadow.

The men, therefore, batched on this last trip into the high mountains. As most of them were good camp cooks, they did not suffer too much for want of good food. Cattle were being pushed out of the mountains each day, and, as on the trip into the mountains, a lot of the stock would continue on their own once they were stirred and started down the trails. Some cows doubtless would get to thinking about the hay stacks on the ranch and go off and leave their calves.

Being near the end of September and October, the men would camp together at Smith's or Robertson's. Staying up late playing cards or talking, with conversation centering around deer hunting, was the most common form of entertainment. Some of the buck stories dated back to the days when Marvin and Stanley were boys hunting in this same country. One such account related how they went out with only a couple of shells each for their 32-Special rifles. Getting a long shot at a large buck, they wounded him, but spent their shells without killing him. Not wanting to leave him badly wounded, and being too late to go to camp for more ammunition, they tracked him down. As the buck lay half dead from loss of blood, the boys crept up on him. The plan was to grab his head and cut his throat before he could do any damage. As it turned out, he had more life in him than they figured. Two hundred pounds of fury was unleashed in the brush patch. It looked bad as the boys hung on for dear life, wanting so much to turn loose. Their faithful old dog, though, came to the rescue and grabbed the buck by the nose, giving them the chance to cut the buck's throat.

One thing that made buck hunting accounts interesting was the fact that most South Forkers hunted deer Indian style. This meant that once they got on a large buck's track, they stuck with it until they had an opportunity to get in a fatal shot. Their forefathers had hunted the same way, having favorite bucks with names such as Geronimo, Pisano, and Club Foot. These bucks were located each year by their tracks, and hunted until they were killed. Each track was different to these old-timers, and each told a story. The bucks' ultimate fates were sealed after they were tracked and put on the list of those worthy of hunting.

A world of hunting knowledge was acquired by these men in a lifetime. Much of it was picked up from the Indians they grew up with, and who were close friends. The rest was acquired by hundreds of hours spent on the tracks of game until they understood how the buck's mind worked, and I think the deer enjoyed it as much as the hunter. Often times, the hunters would kick them out of their beds, and so give them a running chance. And many, such as that master buck hunter, Tommy Smith, never shot them any place but in the neck. Each fall, many friends and relatives would go in for these deer hunts, and the warm bond of friendship that was formed during these yearly hunts is portrayed in the following poem written by Jud Jordan, a close friend of Tommy Smith, when Tommy died in 1921:

IN MEMORY OF MY DEAR FRIEND,
THE LATE THOMAS S. SMITH

The dear old boy has laid aside
His saddle, horse and gun;
The trails that knew his presence once
Are riderless by one.
He drifted out one evening
With an angel by his side
Across the unknown spaces
Beyond the great divide.
He stole away so softly
While the stars their vigil kept,
That those who watched beside him

John Nicoll, a South Fork cattleman and buck hunter.

Scarcely knew but that he slept.
I love you Tommy, dear old boy,
In memory I can see
You riding out across the hills
And beckoning to me.
I see you leading out along
The trails we used to know,
That wound far up among the peaks
And then far down below.
We'll miss you, Companyero,
On the trails we used to know;
We'll miss your smiles and stories
By the campfire's mellow glow.
And when the campfire flickers low
And all the long night through
The stars look down upon your camp—
Oh God, how we'll miss you.
Then when the camp's all quiet
And the 'punchers are at rest,
We'll breathe a prayer for one who rides
Far out beyond the West.
And in our dreams we'll be with you
Upon an antlered track,
And follow it along the hill
Up through the tamarack.
The same old packs will lie around
The camps we used to know;
The same old caviatha
On meadow down below.
The same camp fire'll be burning
In the old accustomed place
With the same boys gathered 'round it,
But there'll be a vacant place.
The same South Fork's still flowing
Through the Rock House Valley sink,
With the same trails leading to it
Where the deer come down to drink.
There's the same old rugged gorge below
With the river roaring through,
Where we've all spent many happy hours
While fishing there with you.
Often, when at Chimney's camp site
Where the red men long ago
Painted on the rocks above it
Characters but red men know,
When the day was slowly dying,
Resting by the campfire's glow
We have talked of these same symbols,
Relics of a long ago.
Dear old boy, these trails still call us
When the autumn time is here;
Call us to the trails we traveled
At the hunting time each year.

We shall always heed the summons,
Just the same as we used to do,
'Till we're called to take the long trail
O'er the great divide to you.

J. H. Jordan<br>Bakersfield, California

Many fine venison steaks and roasts were enjoyed, and the manner in which the game was dressed and cared for made it prime eating. A couple of flour sacks of deer jerky were usually prepared, and a few pieces stuck in a jacket pocket made the stomach more comfortable on many a long ride. Jerky is made by cutting meat in long, narrow strips, and cutting across the grain to make it more tender. Plenty of salt and pepper was used, the pepper being used primarily to keep the flies off. These strips were hung over a wire or cord until dried, and then stored so the air could freely circulate through it. Besides being carried as a snack, a fine gravy and delicious stew were made from either deer or beef jerky.

Often the deer season would end while the cattle were being pushed out through the low country. If a storm hit about the same time, the deer were forced to migrate from the high country. Sometimes, the cowboys happened across a dozen or so big bucks who would just stand and watch them as if they knew perfectly well the season had closed.

The weather at this time of year could change overnight, from sunshine and brilliant fall colors among the quaking aspen and oaks to a blanket of snow on the ground and a howling wind. Camping out was not much fun in rough weather, so special haste was made to get the stragglers down the trail and onto the home ranches.

As the cattle drifted down from the plateau, Stanley Smith usually opened a gate to one of his fields along Highway 178. Every few days, after a fairly large bunch of cattle had collected there, the other cattlemen cut out their stock and took them on to their ranches. A few hurried trips were made back to the mountains to "cut tracks." This was accomplished by riding enough of the country to determine, by recent tracks, if any cattle had been left behind. They would track down those cattle, which, for some reason, had not been chased out by foul weather.

The cattleman's life was not all a bed of roses. A person had to be fitted for this type of work or he would not stay with it. The cattle business has often been said to be more than just a business; it's a way of life. This was certainly so with the South Fork-

Cowboys from the Sprague Ranch, from the left, Rocky Stone, Jim Andreas, Sr. and Jim Andreas, Jr.

A group of the old time cattlemen who neighbored across the Monache drift fence from the Fish Creek permittees, 1968. The occasion was one of Spainhower's annual barbecues on his birthday. At left is Russ Spainhower, Lone Pine cattleman. For many years he furnished most of the wagons and livestock for movie companies during the 1930's and 1950's when they filmed in the Lone Pine and Alabama Hills area. Next is young John Lubken, John H. Lubken (self-proclaimed range boss on the Monache Range), his brother Art Lubken and Mark Lacey (owner of the Double Circle "L" Ranch). Mark was a rancher for over fifty years, as was his father before him. The Monache drift fence was constructed in 1913 to separate the South Fork Kern River cattle from the Lone Pine cattle.

The Olivas cabin in Monache has been the center of hospitality for the last fifty years. Built in 1937 by Henry (Leaky) and Ethel Olivas. From left: Danny Tores, John Lacey, John **Morris,** and Ethel Olivas. When the riders came into sight they could hear Ethel laugh a mile away. She would exclaim, "Here come the boys" and start rattling the stove lids to prepare a big spread.

ers. There were a lot of hot, dusty rides. Cowboys, at times in the desert, got so dry they could not even talk. Water holes were few and far between, and tradition kept them from carrying a water bag or canteen. On fall trips, they almost froze to death, as there was no way to wear enough clothes to keep warm and still be able to work on horseback.

These cattlemen regretted seeing more of the back country opened up each year. The concept of "Multiple Use" was good and the Forest Service was wisely practicing it. The thousands of people who enjoyed the Kern Plateau were also entitled to this wonderful experience of camping in the high country, but to some, the peace and quiet were gone.

These old-timers were not anti-social, but it was hard for them to get used to lining out a bunch of cattle down a trail and having them all come back at you after hearing the roar of a trail bike. Having to untangle a Honda-shy bronc from a bunch of small lodgepole pines made a man wonder if he was not born fifty years too late.

George Brown, a Lone Pine Cattleman.

Ada Brown, George Brown's wife, in **Monache** Meadow. Ada related that every morning the camp would be awakened at 3:00 a.m. by the range boss, John Lubken, hollering at his horse out in the meadow. Everyone had to saddle up by lantern light as it was still dark out. They were always a long way from camp by the time it was daylight.

Frank Chrysler, born on the South Fork of the Kern. He moved to Lone Pine as a boy and lived there the rest of his life. To his right is his friend and neighbor, Russ Spainhower.

Branding crew at a ranch in Lone Pine. From left: Dee Mankin, Bill Carrasco, Con Zuniga, Henry Olivas, Ruby Carrasco, Tom Noland, and Pete Olivas.

Bruce Morgan, a Lone Pine packer.

## THE MONACHE RODEO, 1920

Cattlemen from the South Fork of the Kern River have been neighboring across the Monache drift fence with Inyo County cattlemen from Olancha and Lone Pine for some seventy-four years. Over the years many special friendships have developed between these men and their families. While there have been many informal visits between these two groups, the one that has been mentioned most often over the years by those on both sides of the fence is the rodeo held on July 22, 23 and 24, 1920.

The following newspaper article, taken from the Bakersfield *Californian* and reprinted with their permission, chronicles that memorable occasion. Several have said that the article was written by Charles Andress' sister, Lottie Andress Pettypool, who was a correspondent for the *Californian* during this period. The photographs which follow the article appear courtesy of the Johnny and Ruth Potter family.

### Great Rodeo is Staged in High Mountains; Many Exciting Events
Keen Competition Between Inyo County and South Fork Rough Riders

Kernville August 2, 1920 - The annual three day rodeo held last week at Monache Meadows was an event of unusual interest and pleasure, there being in attendance some 40 South Fork cowboys and cowgirls who had the time of their lives contesting with the Inyo County cattlemen and women. Promoters of the rodeo were the Inyo cattlemen and the well known ranger, George Zeigler, of that locality.

The rodeo was held on an ideal spot, a regular old-time round-up, free from all corrals and fences, every horseman present taking his turn. Those in charge of the affairs were George Zeigler and Mr. Alexander of Inyo County and Mr. A.T. Smith officiating on the finance committee. Acting as judges in all contests were Mr. Skinner, Art Lubkin,

The Monache Rodeo, July 22 and 23, 1920.

**Young Sanford**

Mr. Sears, Mr. Charyo all of Inyo and Charles Andress of Weldon.

The program proper opened with a riding contest in which two South Fork men and three Inyo boys qualified for the finals. Mr. Mackie of Inyo, who rode the South Fork horse known as "Onyx," was immediately qualified for the finals by the judges. Next of the qualifying stunts was a steer riding contest in which two South Fork men and a boy, Buzz Palmer aged 14, and three Inyo men took part, two Inyo and two South Fork boys being appointed to lead out the steers from the herd, while Red Vega of Onyx and Mr. Mackintire of

**From left: Frank Cornett, Charles Andress**

Trout Meadow "put on the bull rigging." The surrounding hills echoed with cheers when little Buzz Palmer rode his steer.

At this point the gong sounded for "chuck" and a most delicious dinner was served on the Cafeteria Plan. All those who ate of the barbecued meat pronounced it the best they had ever eaten.

### Ladies Race

Immediately after dinner the ladies horse races took place — four horses and riders qualifying. The first horse through was Bluebird, ridden by Mrs. Etta Andress of Weldon; second, Ruth Hunter; third, Ruth James and fourth Mrs. Bernhart. This was an extremely interesting race as each rider did her best and saw to it that her horse did likewise.

Next on the program was the roping contest in which Don Hanning of South Fork took first honors by bringing his yearling to a stop in 10 seconds. Many other cowboys, both from Inyo and South Fork, entered this contest, but none could compete with young Hanning.

The mule race was the next stunt. "Wild Joe" from South Fork taking first honors, Charles Summers of Inyo got second by causing the third mule to stampede. The mule and rider went sightseeing over the greater part of Monache.

### Stake Roping Contest

Next was the stake roping contest in which Frank Mendoza was winner. This closed the first day's events. The second day's sport was great, everyone coming early and "rarin" to go. Many more from both sides of the "driftwood fence" were qualified for the finals. John Lubken of Lone Pine, who was appointed cattle rustler, not the moonlight rustler, but just for the occasion, gave South Fork the honors for the best bucking steers.

The final day was opened with loud cheers from both sides of the "driftwood fence."

### Second Day

The program opened with a men's riding contest in which young Sanford of Inyo won first prize; Young Mackie, Art Seals and Jess Smith rode a draw for second prize, each rider drawing his horse's name from slips of paper placed in a hat. Don Hanning drew Onyx, but Art Seals, the expert rider, begged to trade and was granted the privelege of mounting the "wild horse." However, being a brainy little horse, and seeing he had no show to dislodge his rider, Onyx threw down his head and turned a complete somersault pinning Sears to the

Art Seals on Onyx

Buzz Palmer waiting to ride his steer.

ground with horn and cantle board. Although he came off somewhat crippled, he was no less the victor, for as a surprise to Onyx he remounted the brute and conquered him so completely that he is decidedly a better and wiser animal. Jess Smith of South Fork put up a nice clean ride on Sleepy Dick, sticking him with the spurs and at the same time brushing away the flies with his hat.

## Steer Riding

The next event was the steer riding contest in which Harold Gill was given first prize on the strength of his having ridden his steer to a finish even after his boots were bucked off. Jess Smith took second money.

Next was a roping contest in which Don Hanning swept the stake, bettering his former time by one second. Frank Comett (Cornett?) of Inyo won second money in 10.2-5 seconds. The rest of the ropers couldn't catch a doughnut with a skimmer.

The next contest was a parting out cattle contest. Bev Hunter and Frank Comett(Cornett?) contesting against Red Vega and Charles Andress. The Inyo boys won by eight seconds.

## Final Contest

The final contest for the ladies race came next and was the most exciting event of the rodeo.

Mrs. Vivian Frederick of South Fork took first prize on Cremo, while Mrs. Etta Andress took second on Bluebird. Ruth James Potter and Ruth Hunter ran so close that the judges could not give a decision.

Turning the sod, the three stake race was won by Mark Lacey in 19.4-5 seconds. The tie was run off, Andress winning by making a record of 19 seconds flat.

Jimmie Ross saved the South Forkers a long walk home by winning the foot race against young Crocker, which he won by a small margin. The South Forkers last cent was bet on him.

## Short Address

The three days rodeo was concluded with a short address by Charles Andress, in which he expressed the gratitude of the South Fork people for the

Riders and Judges.

93

kindness and courtesy shown them by the Inyo people. Mr. George Zeigler promptly responded a hearty invitation to meet them again next year. The big hearted Charles Summers invited the South Forkers to his camp for supper.

The crowning event was the open air dance in the evening. By the light of enormous bon-fires the assembly danced till 12 o'clock, when a sumptuous supper was served.

The South Fork boys claim all honors as "ladies men" as they won the favor of every "schoolma'am" in Monache.

**Charlie Summers**

# Memories of the ZX Ranch

In 1947, after the calf branding had been completed on the Fish Creek Range, the author decided he wanted to try cowboying on a new range. For years I had wanted to work for the Kern County Land Company, so I went to Bakersfield to talk to Clint McCray about a job. Clint was a manager of the company's cattle operation in California. He was also a family friend who had been raised in the Kern River Valley. Clint told me that they were "full up" in California, but if I didn't mind going to Oregon, I could get work on the company's ZX Ranch at Paisley. The ranch manager in Oregon at that time was Buster Vaughn, who had also worked on the Kern River for Jack Doyle. This suited me fine.

Bob Powers in 1947 when he was ready to leave the Valley for the ZX Ranch in Oregon.

I loaded my worldly possessions in my '41 Chevy club coupe and off I went. These possessions amounted to the following: two saddles, the first a Brydon Brothers single rig bronc saddle, and a Fred Muller double ring roping saddle; a sack of assorted horse gear, such as chaps, bridles, spurs; and, of course, my bed roll, the forerunner of the sleeping bag. Cowboys in those days carried most of their spare clothes in what we called a war bag. Mine was a heavy canvas sea bag I had been issued in the navy. I had three blue work shirts, two pairs of work Levis (neither of which I washed—one pair for regular work, the other for dirty work, such as branding), two Pendleton dress shirts, an assortment of underwear, including long handles, which many cowboys wore year round, and extra socks. I also carried a pair of dress boots and a new pair of Levis for dress. I had a light work jumper and a heavier coat, along with a slicker for stormy weather. This made up my wardrobe and could all be packed away in my war bag. In another small canvas bag, I carried my tooth brush, razor (which I didn't use while in Oregon), and other toilet articles.

Outside of my bed roll and clothes, the only other thing I remember having with me was a portable wind-up phonograph and three Ernest Tubbs records. After playing these over and over for a few weeks, I had to hide them, as the others would have gladly broken them if they had gotten their hands on them. They never did know I had hidden them under the floor mats in my car.

When I arrived in Paisley, I gave Buster Vaughn a letter from Clint McCray. Buster said both wagons were out already, but if I didn't mind driving my car out to where one wagon was on the Sycan Marsh, I could go to work the next day. I started out early the next morning. Because it was towards the end of the summer, the marsh was fairly well dried up. There were no signs along the way, and after getting a little lost a few times and hitting high center a couple of times, I finally made it to camp just before dark, but still in time for the evening meal.

I wouldn't take any amount of money for my experiences the next few months. I met the crew I was to spend twenty-four hours a day with for the next three months. They called this the Boy Wagon. The Jigger Boss, Wayne Heller, known as Lopey, was the oldest at twenty-five. I was twenty-three at that time, and the other five on the wagon were all under twenty, the youngest being the horse wrangler who was fourteen. The term "Wild Bunch" has been used many times, but it would also fit this crew to a "T."

Wayne "Lopey" Heller, 1949, ZX Ranch. He later became cow-boss of the Squaw Valley Ranch, a job he still held in 1982. In 1987 Lopey was **retired and living in Yerington, Nevada. In 1981** his son, Twister, was working on the D.A. Ranch in Arizona. There is a lot of cowboy in this family.

Joe Herin on Sailor. Taken in 1949 at the Black Hills Camp on the Klamath Indian Reservation, ZX Ranch. The author misplaced his pictures over the years, but Joe kept his set and shared them to use in *Cowboy Country*.

Lopey Heller on the rubber tired chuck wagon, as it was being loaded for the last time, in the fall of 1947. The next year the ranch had a one-ton truck made into a chuck wagon. Note the stove fastened on the back and the wash tub, or wreck pan, tied above it. When the six bronco mules broke into a dead run across the rough marsh the tub banging made them run all the faster.

The outfit had only recently had a new chuck wagon built, and this was the one I rode with. It was modern enough to have rubber tires, but in all other ways was the traditional chuck wagon. It had a good-sized wood cook stove that was fastened up on the back of the wagon when it was moved. When camp was set up, there was a work counter that hinged down from the back of the wagon; this also served as the lid for the chuck box. A couple of legs folded down, and at the end of this work counter, the stove was set up. The back of the wagon was fitted with cupboards that held camp utensils, along with flour, sugar, and spices. There was a tent that fastened to the back of the wagon, and this was the kitchen. There was a small table and one chair for the cook; everyone else sat on the ground. There were hooks on the side of the wagon where the beef was hung out each night to cool. During the day, it was wrapped in meat sacks, old quilts,

Six cowboys hold the mules until they are hooked up and the driver gets in his place on the box. In the far left you can catch a glimpse of Bob's 1941 Chev.

Kern County Land Company Ranch near Seligman, Arizona. Known as the Boquillas Cattle Company in 1950. The brands used were Diamond A, Wagon Rod, and the Three V. In the background 5,200 head of two and three year old steers. Back row from left: Wayne Halloway, Cherokee Sessions (horse wrangler), Jack Halloway, Everett McCauley, Pappy Prather, Tom Cook, Carl Welch. In front from the left, Pete Conners, Leland Larson (superintendent), Boaz Haver (wagon boss), Ken Rhoads, and Marion Ducenburger. (Photo, courtesy Ken Rhoads.)

A bunch of the boys from the Boquillas East Wagon on the 3V Ranch eating breakfast around the fire. From left: Don Manis, Marion Ducenburger, Cherokee Sessions, Boaz Haver, Pappy Prather, Wayne Halloway, Pete Conners, unidentified Hoodlum Wagon driver (bed wagon), Carl Welch, Ken Rhoads, and Everett McCauley. (Photo, courtesy Ken Rhoads.) **97**

and canvas, and put under the wagon out of the sun. The cook had an outside fire built that always had a coffee pot going on it, but most of the cooking was done in the cook tent.

On the boy wagon, there was always a lot of horsing around in camp after work was done. We got up early, about 4:30 a.m., and on most days we were through by 3:30 or 4:00 in the afternoon. There were always two or three of the young guys who kept things hopping until well after dark. There would be wrestling matches, frog races, and all kinds of tricks played on each other. I added to the confusion by playing my three Ernest Tubb records non-stop on my wind-up phonograph.

Although we got hardly any days off, we did make three or four runs into Klamath Falls. We convinced Lopie, the wagon boss, that as long as we were back for breakfast and able to work the next day, it would be O.K. This didn't happen many times over the years because, as a rule, they didn't allow any of the cowboys to keep their own transportation out with the wagon. Of course, the country was too rough most of the time to make it practical. Six of us would pile into my Chevy, leaving only the wagon boss, horse wrangler, and cook in camp. We bounced across the marsh until we got to a logging road. It was a two hour trip each way, driving mostly on dusty logging roads. When we arrived in town, we would get one room so we could take showers and put on our clean clothes. We would roam around town looking at the bright lights until everything closed down, and drive back to camp just in time to see the cook lighting his lantern in preparation for starting breakfast.

Breakfast was usually a big meal. There were always either sourdough pancakes or biscuits. I would have to say that the cook's sourdough culinary skills were hard to beat. He was very particular about his sourdough keg. One evening something happened concerning this keg that I didn't dare tell the rest of the crew about. The cook told us when we finished eating there was a bowl of tapioca pudding in the cook tent. I was the first through eating, and as it was about dusk and there wasn't a lantern burning in the tent, I had a little trouble finding the pudding. As I tried to dish it up, I remembered thinking it was awfully sticky and didn't dish up like any pudding I had ever had. I went out and squatted down by the fire to eat my pudding. I never even got the first bite down. It was the sourest pudding I had ever eaten. I was lucky enough to find a gopher hole to stuff it down without anyone seeing me.

ZX Wagon Cook, Elmer Shultz, lets a few of the cowboys in out of the cold fall weather. From left: Ray Boch, Dean Cannon, Lopey Heller, Will Glen.

The next one to look for the pudding was smart enough to ask the cook where to find it. They all said how good it was. I thought to myself, they were sure afraid to say what they really thought. I didn't say anything; I never was that good of a liar. The next morning, the cook woke us up bellowing that someone had been messing with his sourdough starter. I didn't dare tell anyone what had happened because they were just the kind of guys to tell the cook and he would probably have chased me clear off the Sycan Marsh. We would have bacon, ham or sausage each morning, along with fried potatoes. Some days the cook would fry up some steaks for breakfast, and when he did, he would make gravy in the pans after the steaks were done.

About mid-day, the horse wrangler would drive the cavvy out to where we were working cattle so we could rope out fresh horses. Usually we didn't stop for a noon meal. As a general rule, breakfast was at 5:00 a.m. and the second meal at 4:00 in the evening, but sometimes we did eat three meals a day.

Beef was always the center of the evening meal. Although the cook sometimes fried steaks for breakfast, meat for the night meal was usually baked in the oven. We killed a good young beef about every three weeks and shared it with the other wagon and the crew at the Thompson place.

Besides the experience of camping and working out of a chuck wagon, the next most exciting thing was the horses they gave us to ride. The ranch had a caviatha of about two hundred head. Each man was given a string of fifteen horses. They would keep up five head for each man and the rest would be

In front of cook tent - ZX Ranch 1947. The tent is fastened to the wagon just beyond the stove pipe. Bud Stevens, Shirley Herin, Joe Herin, and **Ray Boch**, horse wrangler, standing by tent flap. Bob Powers seated outside cook tent, where he got into the cook's sour dough starter. Note dish towels drying on the tent ropes.

turned in the Reservation Field, an area covering several sections. We would ride the five head for two weeks, then gather the Reservation Field and run the horse herd into a big corral at the Thompson place. We would then rope out five fresh horses and turn the ones we had been riding back into the herd. I have heard several different cowboys say that after riding for big outfits all over the West, the ZX Ranch definitely had more mean, spoiled horses than any other place they had worked. I haven't worked on many ranches, but those horses

on the XZ, as a whole, had about all the bad habits I have ever heard about. Prior to my arrival at the ranch, two bronc riders by the names of Dollerhide and Blasingame had started horses there. Many times I heard the boys use their names in connection with a string of cuss words that questioned the horses' ancestors. I doubt that it was the fault of the horse breakers, but was due mostly to the fact that the horses would be turned out sometimes several months after being started. They might then be given to one of the young cowboys who came to

ZX Cowboys Sycan Marsh, 1947. From left: Shirley Herin, Joe Herin, Ray Boch, Bill Ray (who in 1987 was cattle inspector in French Camp, California), Lopey Heller, Roy Wildman, Warren Miles, Bob Powers on Rex (this big bay horse weighed 1,600 pounds and wore number five shoes), Bill "Red" Mosslander, Ben Crowley, Johnny Miller, Bud Stevens.

Dean Cannon on Tango in 1947. Dean was the first member of the crew the author contacted after 40 years. Cannon still had the 25 colt automatic which I traded to him in '47.

ZX Cowboys - Sycan Marsh, 1947. On horseback from left: Johnny Miller and Bud Stevens. On ground, Bob Powers, Joe Herin, Lopey Heller, and Ray Boch. Other cowboys who rode on the ZX from '47 to '49 not pictured in *Cowboy Country* are Ben Crowley, Joe Silvera, Claude Harris, George "Boots" Menkenaier, "Over the River" Charlie Harvey, Blackie Fowler, and Bill Lane.

work on the outfit. Many of these boys wanted to be bronc riders, and many times would encourage the young horses to buck, if the horses didn't do it on their own. Sometimes we would get away from camp without a horse bucking, but not very often. When one started, three or four others would break in two also, encouraged by aspiring rodeo hands.

The bad habits these horses had ran the gamut, all the way from falling over backwards to striking and kicking a cowboy whenever they could. Some were extremely hard to mount. In my string, there was one horse by the name of Congo that could only be mounted by tying up the off front foot and

getting on him while he was standing on three legs. These horses that were hard to get on acted like they had been broke with blinds. (A blind is a wide strip of leather fastened to the headstall that you pulled down over a horse's eyes before you got on him. After you were on, you leaned over and pulled it up so he could see.) The horses were all broken to be caught only by being roped. You could not walk up to any horse on the outfit and catch him without first tossing a loop over his head. They were also accustomed to being hobbled before being saddled. You couldn't get blankets or saddles on them without first hobbling them.

There had been so many Southern boys working

ZX Branding Crew, 1949. From left: Will Glen horseback, Tom McCoy, Buster Vaughn on Pinkey, Joe Silvera, Rich Bradbury, cow-boss, standing behind branding crew. Harold Gill back to camera. Pop Pate, who worked for the ZX over 30 years, wearing white hat. Tom Bratton in checked coat; seated with white hat "Soapy" Bob, wagon cook.

Catching horses in a rope corral. Kern County Land Company Ranch, Seligman, Arizona, in 1950. Ken Rhoads saddling his horse in the background. (Photo, courtesy Ken Rhoads.)

on the ranch over the past ten years that tied hard to the horn instead of taking their dallies (taking several turns around the saddle horn after a catch had been made). Because of this, when you took a swing to take your dallies, the horse thought you were attempting to beat him on the head and started dodging and ducking his head. I had only two horses in my string that were good to rope calves on, as I was a dally man. Only two other cowboys out of the total of eighteen men from the two wagons used the dally method when roping instead of tying their rope hard and fast to the horn.

We branded about 500 head of calves while camped there on the Marsh. The wagon boss asked if any of us had castrated many bull calves, and I said I had. I was given the job. One of the old-timers, Warren Miles, and myself did all the castrating. He and I took turns, when he was working on the ground I would be roping calves, and every so often we traded off. I sure was glad I had that job, because it was, by far, the easiest. We had a lot of big calves, some almost yearlings, and as you dragged them up to the fire by one or two hind feet, a pair of flankers grabbed them and held them down as one cowboy put his weight on a front shoulder and pulled a front leg up and back while holding his knee down on the calf's shoulders. The

other part of the team grabbed the hind leg that was off the ground and sat down behind the calf. By placing a foot on the back of the calf's leg just above the hock, he forced the leg forward to keep him from kicking. It usually worked, unless you got kicked in the process of getting into position. With smaller calves, it was fairly easy, but with the bigger calves, I have seen a lot of skin taken off the cowboys when they got kicked or scraped with one of those three inch stub horns. On top of that, the man in back was sitting right down on the ground. After having several hundred cows milling around the corral, the ground was anything but clean!

If we were cutting yearlings or day cows from the herd and had a real big bunch of cattle, the wagon boss would have the horse wrangler bring the saddle string out and we would pen them up, using our lass ropes. They would stand real good in a pen made of ropes held waist high, because they had been broke that way. We would rope out a fresh horse and put the ones we had been riding back into the cavvy.

The other wagon that was out had ten men on the crew, all older men from thirty-five to the oldest, Warren Miles, who was sixty-nine at that time. It was a wise move on the part of management to keep the two age groups split up. For a month or more, the two wagons were camped about a mile apart, and many days the whole eighteen men worked together. When the work was done, each group went to their own camp.

I remember Warren Miles, Sr. as if it were yesterday when I rode with him, instead of forty years ago. He still carried his weight; nothing too fancy, but just a steady, dependable old cowboy, although Mr. Miles, as all the young men called him, had been on the ZX for twenty-two years.

I didn't know it at the time, but the list of his employers for the thirty-eight years prior to his coming to the ZX Ranch read like a list of "Who's Who" of famous cattle barons of the West. I found out about Mr. Miles' early life many years after I rode with him in 1947. I belong to the Western Writers of America, and when I sat down to read the January 1983 issue of *The Roundup* (published ten times a year by this organization), I really got a surprise. I started reading an article by Robert Bell, a Western Writer's member. It was entitled, "Chip Miles of the Flying U." As I read this interesting account, I kept glancing at the picture on the second page of the article and wondering where I had seen the picture. When I read that Miles had gone to work for the ZX Ranch at Paisley, Oregon, in 1925, I realized all of a sudden I hadn't seen the picture, but the man, and had worked with him thirty-six years ago.

Warren A. Miles, Sr. had been born in Sherman, Texas on July 7, 1878. According to Robert Bell, Miles got his first job as horse wrangler for Colonel Jack Potter, the legendary Indian fighter, preacher, and cattleman. Miles, who was only nine at the time but big for his age, passed himself off as "going on" sixteen. Miles' first job on a cattle drive was for Abe and John Blocker as they trailed the cattle north to Wyoming Territory. This job led to employment on the XIT Ranch that covered more than three million acres in nine counties in Texas. By this time, Miles was only eleven. The huge XIT started splitting up. He then worked for Charley Goodnight, a spread on the Quitaque in southeast Briscoe County, Texas. When, in 1890, Goodnight decided to sell the J. A. Ranch, Miles was ready to see some new country. In between working on cattle ranches and drifting around the country, he married a girl by the name of Alice and they had four children. In 1925, he loaded his family and belongings in his Model T Ford and headed north to Oregon. Miles took a job on the ZX Ranch near Paisley. He realized he had traveled

**Warren Miles on Comanche, Syncan Marsh 1947. The boys on the ZX called Miles "Molly" because of his incessant whistling of "Molly and Me."**

around enough and the ZX was a good place to stop.

Andy Charlton was the buckaroo boss on the ZX in 1925 when Miles arrived. Over sixty years later, Andy remembers how Miles came into the bunk house with his bed on his shoulder, threw it down and proclaimed, "Well, boys, I've come to stay." He found comfortable housing there for his family, stayed, and watched them marry and have children of their own.

Andy recalled that Miles was a good, reliable hand. While not the dashing figure some might associate with the old time cowboy, he was just a good all-around hand who was at his best calving out first-calf heifers or camped out in a line camp seeing to it that the cattle stayed on the range that they were supposed to be on. When you told him to do something, he did everything in his power to do it your way. This type of dependability is still very important today. Miles never swore, and the closest to using cuss words when he got mad was to exclaim, "Well, I'll be John Brown!"

Miles rode for the ZX until 1953 and had spent sixty-seven years on horseback, when, because of poor health, he hung up his saddle. He passed away in his sleep three years later at seventy-eight.

I met Andy Charlton first in 1985. I had heard that he had worked for the ZX Ranch, so I paid him a visit. He was living just across the valley from me with his daughter, Ann, and her husband, Dr. Detlev Lange. Lange operates the Kern Valley Veterinary Clinic. It was like old home week as I talked with Andy about the ZX. Not that much had changed as far as how the ranch was operated from when Andy was there in the 20's and 30's and when

I worked there in 1947. The difference was, when he was there the ranch ran about 20,000 head of mother cows, and when I got there they had cut down to about 10,000 head of cows. He talked about how tough the horses were and how there were cowboys in the air all the time. Riding with the chuck wagon was then, and still is, not much different from what it was in the 1870's and '80's.

Andy was born in New Pine Creek, Oregon, in 1900, but left home at fifteen and headed for Arizona. Andy's father and grandfather had both been cattlemen, and at a young age, he was riding for the Mares Ranch. He also worked for the Wineglass outfit in southeastern Nevada, the C. S. Ranch out of Winnemucca, Nevada, the Miller and Lux at the San Emigdo, and the Poso Ranch. After working on quite a few more outfits in Arizona, New Mexico, and Nevada, Andy ended up in the South Fork Valley working for the Onyx Ranch. The year was 1922, and when one of Andy's friends by the name of Lewis Smith came by on his way to the ZX Ranch, Andy decided to go along. Andy had worked for Smith on the Diamond A's in Arizona when Smith was wagon boss there. Another friend by the name of Butch Smith, who also had worked as wagon boss on that same Kern County Land Company Ranch in Arizona, was sent to the ZX Ranch as superintendent. Another cowboy by the name of Buster Vaughn was working for the Onyx Ranch and he went along to Oregon with Andy. Frank Berens, who had been working for the Bakersfield Police Department, also wanted to go back to cowboying, so he went along, too. While they were in Oregon, Butch Smith died and Buster Vaughn was given the job of superintendent, a job he held until he decided to leave the ranch. Vaughn was still the superintendent when I arrived in 1947.

People who work livestock from horseback have been notorious for at least the last 150 years for not wanting to do any kind of work that couldn't be done from the back of a horse, unless it was something like taking their turn on the ground during calf branding.

When Zenas Leonard was out in California in 1833-34 with Captain Joseph Walker, he told how

Cowboys leaving Onyx for the ZX Ranch in Oregon in the winter of 1921. From left: Frank Berens, Buster Vaughn, Andy Charlton, and Louis Smith.

the vaqueros hated to do anything on foot. He wrote in his diary,* "They appear to do most of their work on horseback. If they want wood, they repair to the forest, ride along until they find a log to suit them, then they drop their noose around the end of it and, thus, drag it to their homes. They are very expert on horseback, nor could it be otherwise, for they are constantly riding and never appear so well satisfied as when they are seated on a prancing steed."

Andy said, himself, that he had always preferred to work for the big outfits because all you had to do was ride and didn't have to do any of the other ranch jobs. He also told about one of the crews he had while he was buckaroo boss. They had to pitch hay for ten days. It happened this way. March first was the normal date to turn the cows out on the spring range. Working as buckaroo boss, Andy had a herd of 3,500 cows ready to take to the desert. He had his crew of fourteen men and the wagon all ready; however, the night before it snowed a foot. Andy went to the ranch boss, Dave Dodson, and asked him if he had hay for the cows until the snow

*Adventures of Zenas Leonard, Fur Trader, edited by John C. Ewers.

melted. He said he did, but had turned all his hay pitchers loose. He could furnish men to load the wagons, but didn't have anyone to pitch the hay off. Andy told how he got his crew together and told them, "Now, you boys are all here and you're getting paid, but you know we can't go to the desert until the snow melts. Dodson said he can load the wagons for us, but you will have to pitch it off. If you don't want to feed cattle, you can draw your pay." Andy said they didn't like it too well, but they all agreed to stay.

Two of the men who had been working on the haying crew loaded seven large hay wagons using a Jackson Fork (a large, six-tined fork powered by a team of horses). With two men to each wagon, one to drive the team and one to pitch the hay off, they fed 600 tons of loose hay in ten days. When Andy was lining out his crew to feed, he put all the lazy men together and the good workers together. This prevented a man who didn't care for manual labor from driving the team everyday and thus letting a good worker pitch all the hay off. He said they tried to change around so that they could work with somebody who would do their share of hay pitching too, but he wouldn't let them.

Each wagon had its own crew, consisting of cook, wrangler and cowboys. This is one wagon crew at the Jones Place, ZX Ranch, in the early 1920's. From left: Red Morris, Andy Charlton, Cy Elliot, Niel Fields, Louis Gill and Dick Swartz, one of the best camp cooks ever seen.

Leaving the old Buckaroo Camp at the Jones place in the spring of the early 1920's, because water was beginning to flood around the house. Andy Charlton on the horse by the mules. The horse he rides was called Frog and was one of the best horses Andy ever rode on the ZX. Dick Swartz is on the wagon, Louis Gill on the white horse, and Cy Elliot and Niel Fields.

When the snow melted off and they could take the cows to the desert, never was a crew of cowboys more ready to get back on their horses.

Andy told about other bunches of dry cows his crew took to the spring and summer range. He took one bunch of 6,500 dry cows to the desert one time using just fourteen cowboys.

The night before starting out, they camped at Red Cabin. The first two or three miles, they had to fight the cows every step of the way. Then they realized where they were going and lined out. Andy said the leaders arrived where they were going to camp the first night by noon that day. The distance they covered the first day was twenty miles. The cows were used to going each year to the desert where they had their calves, and once they got started, all the men had to do was ride along with them. Of course, there were always a few stragglers in the drag that had to be driven all the way.

The wagon had gone ahead of the herd to a predetermined spot. At ten o'clock, the cook had lunch fixed for the men and they stopped to eat.

The winters were extremely cold. Andy told me about being out with his crew and several thousand cows and calves between Harney and Paisley when it got down to 40° below zero. The men were sleeping in teepees, but some of them had to night herd the bunch each night. The men spent most of their night shift pulling up sagebrush for a fire to try to stay warm. One night, Frank Barrons came out to relieve Andy and told him, "Why don't you just hop in my bed when you get back to camp? It's all warmed up." When Andy started to get in Frank's bed, he found the blankets frozen stiff at the top of the bed where his friend's breath had hit the blankets. He decided to go warm up his own bed.

One good thing about cold weather was that the horses that normally bucked never gave them any problem. It was just too cold for them to. Some nights, as they tried to stay warm around the fire, some of the little calves from the herd would crowd up around the fire to try to get warm, too. The old cows were pretty smart when it came to protecting their calves against the cold. Where they were holding the cows and calves was on some natural hay meadows. The meadow hay had been cut during the summer and pushed up in bunches with buckrakes. Along the meadows there were quite a few tules, so the hay had tules in it. As the cows were turned in on these piles of hay, they ate almost everything except the tules. On these cold nights, many of the cows would have their calves almost completely buried in what was left of these hay stacks. One time when they kicked the cows off the bed ground, two of the cows failed to get up. Upon checking, they found they had frozen to death and were, in fact, frozen solid. Now, that's too cold! It was stories such as this that made me head back to California and the South Fork Valley when it started getting cold in the fall.

Packing up to leave Sand Springs, a desert camp on the ZX Ranch, in the early 1920's. On the wagon is the cook, Andy Cox; packing horse is Andy Charlton, Louis Gill, and an unidentified cowboy.

Andy said that when he was there in the early Thirties, there was a family by the name of Hannan living in Lakeview that had five daughters. The mother had given her girls specific instructions, "If you get in town and the ZX cowboys are there, you head right home!" Well, this didn't work too well, because one night at a dance in Lakeview, Rita Hannan met Andy Charlton, and in 1932, they were married. The mother didn't have much better luck with her other daughters, as four of the five all married ZX cowboys.

Like I said before, not much had changed in Oregon from the days that Andy had been there. When I arrived, the townspeople of Lakeview and Paisley still didn't want their daughters going out with ZX cowboys. The only time we ever got any days off was when they gave us three days to go to the Lakeview Rodeo. When the other ZX cowboys and myself went to the dance, some of the mothers wouldn't let their daughters even dance with us.

The universal practice of getting the cowboys up at four in the morning was accepted procedure. Andy said if there wasn't much to do, they didn't get up until five. The main reason for getting up early was the cattle worked so much better in the morning. One hour in the morning was worth three hours in the afternoon. Most days, you would get in early in the afternoon, and sometimes you didn't do anything after that.

All cowboys who ever rode with a wagon re-member the good cooks. Andy said Andy Cox was one of the best. One time when Dick Swartz was the cook, he took a short cut over Juniper Hill. The chuck wagon turned over, but Andy said the beans didn't spill. They were frozen solid. Swartz was known for not getting his beans cooked enough, and they always rattled in the pan. They were only using four mules to each chuck wagon, and every time they went over Juniper Hill, six cowboys had to put ropes on and help the team out. Andy added another team, and when I worked with the wagon, they still had six mules pulling it. I never will forget helping harness those six bronco mules. As we hooked them up, a cowboy held each mule until the cook got on the seat and hollered, "Let her go." Off they went in a dead run, the washtub banging against the back of the wagon. Our new cook said he had driven mules all of his life. I think it was down a cotton row, because when the team slowed down at the first gate, he asked Wayne Heller to have one of the cowboys drive and he got off and walked the rest of the way to where they were going to camp.

The cowboy headquarters was at Jones Place, and sometimes there were as many as four wagons out at one time. The biggest bunch Andy ever handled was when they took 7,500 head of dry cows to the desert at one time.

Every cowboy has a few special horses in his life. A little horse called Dinky Dan was Andy's

Cook wagon packed with bed rolls and gear leaving for Lachelle Wells in March of the early 1920's. First day to Lost Cabin, where there was a big pasture and water. Second day to Juniper Mountain, where cattle were guarded all night. The next day to Lachelle Wells where a six inch pipe of running water from a spring filled two big tanks. They would let the cattle water in small bunches and they would drink the tanks dry. They had all kinds of good mules at the ZX Ranch. Most cook wagons at that time had four mules on a wagon. With just four mules, four cowboys had to put ropes on the wagon and help pull it up Juniper Mountain. Six mules could pull the wagon easily. Andy Charlton started this practice and it was still being done when the author was on the ZX Ranch.

A cowboy crew camped at Red House just before leaving for the desert from ZX Ranch. As many as eight crews would camp here when leaving for the desert. Second from the left is Andy Charlton, third from the left is Les Morgan. Louis Gill is at the far right with the black hat barely visible. It was always recognizable because he was getting bald and never took off his black hat where anyone could see him. Note the cowboy tepee tents and how the tarp comes off the back of the cook wagon with the stove set up. Red House is in the background.

favorite. He was a top cutting horse and a cow just couldn't get away from him. When the ground was frozen and slippery and a cow would duck away fast, Dinky Dan would just look the other way. He wasn't about to turn quick and fall down. One time, they were going to ride some country that had a lot of barbed wire scattered around, left from an old homestead. Andy left Dan at Sycan Marsh, as he didn't want to take the chance of getting him cut. When he got back to the Marsh, the first thing he saw was Dinky Dan's four legs sticking up in the air. While he was gone, his top horse had eaten some poison parsnips.

Andy left the ZX Ranch in 1934. The longest he worked on one ranch was for the Rankin Ranch in Walker Basin. He worked there twenty years, first for Leroy Rankin, and after he passed away, for his wife, Helen. It was while Andy was working there that his wife, Rita, had their two children, Ann and Biff.

A lot of Andy's reminiscing had to do with the good cowboys he had worked with over the years, such as Walker Rankin, Jr. What impressed Andy the most about Walker was his honesty. He would never put his mark on another man's calf, even if it had left its mother and nobody would know the difference. There are still a few of those old-time cowboys riding on the big outfits. Every so often, you will read an article about someone like Tom Blasingame, who, at 89, still rides for the J. S. Ranch in Palo Duro Canyon in Texas. There is a whole crowd of those old boys that you will never be able to match; cowboys like Vick Phillips, Andy Charlton, Clifford Cross, and Tip Tipton, Sr.

Butch Smith, Superintendent of the ZX Ranch from the early 1920's until his death. Andy Charlton at right.

Andy Charlton on Dinky Dan at the ZX Ranch.

Warren Rankin, a Walker Basin cattleman.

Bob Whitlock in the 1950's when he came to Weldon to work for Andy Brown. He had previously worked for Brown in Ventura.

A group of old time cowboys at the Andreas cow-camp in Big Meadow. From left: Johnny Johnson, Chris Wirth, Ramon Bencoma, Ernest Andress, Mr. Trawver, and Charlie Andress.

The Milligan Brothers head for the High Country in 1940. Bill (right) with Ray. Ray later became a well-known artist, painting under the name of Clint Worlds.

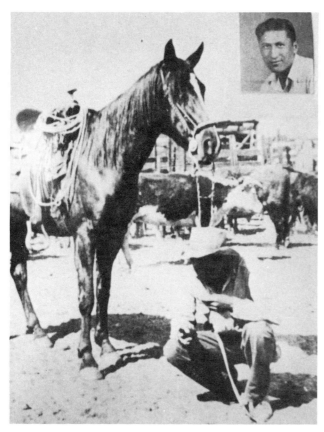

Vic Gomez, riding for the A. Brown Ranch in the early 1930's.

Ray Waters, a long time cowboy for the A. Brown Ranch.

Amos Petersen, South Fork rancher in the 1920's, at the old N.P. Petersen Ranch.

111

John (left) and Bud Silicz on the South Fork in 1940.

Bev. Robinson, Sr., a South Fork cattleman, displays some bells used on the early Jerkline teams in the Kern River Valley.

From left: Roberta Joughin, her daughter Sylvia, with her husband Bruce Hafenfeld. Seated are their children Jessica Louise and Eric Joughin. (Photo by Casey Christie.)

Tony Cain, at the Alexander calf branding in Kennedy Meadows, 1987.

Bill Joughin, Kern River rancher and land developer, stands on his property where he relocated after the waters of Lake Isabella covered most of his old ranch.

The Kissack Ranch crew. From left: Shannon Tuttle, Bill Kissack, Arthur Esponda, Ann Tuttle, and Scott Kissack, the fourth generation to work cattle in the Kern River Valley. (Photo by Casey Christie.)

# My Days on the Onyx Ranch

During my early years, I rode a few colts; some we had raised on the ranch. But as I grew into a teenager, I still didn't feel as if I had a system of bringing a colt along as he should be to give him a chance to make a top cow horse. My dad had been crippled with arthritis early in his life, so he wasn't able to help much in my learning experiences.

Because of this, in 1948 when Wink Chappell, who was the cattle boss for the Onyx Ranch, asked me if I wanted a job riding colts for the outfit, I jumped at the chance. Wink knew I had just come back from riding for the ZX Ranch in Oregon, so called and offered me the job. I asked Wink if he would work with me for a couple of days to make sure I was handling the colts the way he wanted. The truth was, I threw out what little I knew about starting colts and tried to copy his methods.

Wink had worked on the Onyx Ranch, which was just a mile up the road from our ranch, for the past sixteen years. He knew I wasn't any great shakes of a bronc rider, but gave me a chance. Bill Chappell, or Wink as everybody called him, came from a long line of horse trainers. Wink and his Uncle Farrell Chappell and three of his cousins who worked on the Onyx Ranch had come to the Valley from Tehachapi. All of these men, as well as Wink's dad, Bill, Sr., had worked for years for Russell Hill on the Bear Mountain Ranch near Tehachapi. Wink had been breaking horses for Hill seven years before he came to the South Fork.

The Hill Ranch ran about 250 head of mares and kept fifteen stallions. There were five men halter-breaking yearling colts, five men starting green broncs, and ten men who did nothing but bit horses to the Spanish bit. They raised mostly Morgan horses, and a lot of their geldings were shipped back to Chicago for the police department. They

Wink Chappell in 1940 with his dog, Tippy. Wherever Wink went he was like the Pied Piper with eight or ten dogs following him.

Leonard Alexander with his roping horse in 1987. Leonard is a top roper whether in the roping arena or branding corral.

wanted only solid blacks. The ranch would guarantee the horses to be sound and completely broken or the police department would ship them back to California.

When I started riding colts for the Onyx Ranch, I was given five head of green colts and two that had been started previously and were pretty spoiled. One of the colts was a horse called Skunk. This horse was really the reason the job was open at that time. Leonard Alexander had been riding colts for Onyx, and Skunk had bucked him off and broken his shoulder. The same horse had chased Leonard out of the corral once. Wink told how Leonard, not looking, just bailed over the fence and landed on Wink's back as he was bending over hobbling another colt.

I got along pretty well with the first year colts, but Skunk and another big sorrel mare, who had been started the year before, gave me a few bad moments. One of these bad moments came when I was working a big mare we called Lulu. One of the things we did to gentle the colts was to hobble them, both in front and behind, with sack hobbles (hobbles made with a rolled up barley sack that had been cut at the seams). The front and back hobbles were tied together with a short rope. This method is sometimes called using Oklahoma hobbles. As

On the Hill Ranch near Tehachapi. George Archer (left) and grandfather Ed Chappell, who was a pony express rider. Ed also drove stage coach in southern California and worked on many of the early ranches in California. On Ed's right, son Dan Chappell.

116

A bunch of Onyx cowboys in the early 1940's. From left: Glenn Alexander, Ed Chappell, Johnny Chappell, Wink Chappell and Farrel Chappell.

ble jumping out of the way. After a half hour of this, the colt would start to quiet down and you could eventually slide off over its tail and throw your feet up around the colt's ears without too much of a blowup.

Things didn't work too well when I was going through this procedure with Lulu. She had thrown herself several times and seemed to be gentling down pretty well. When I threw one foot up around one of her ears, she jumped straight up, at the same time threw her front legs out to the left side, and as she came down, she spun to the left. Being used to getting on and off on the left side, I had jumped off on that side. I rammed my right leg, clear to the knee, right between the front hobbles. My weight was enough to cause her to stumble and fall. I had the good luck to grab her by one ear and her nose. The big old mare was putting a lot of pressure on me as we thrashed around on the ground, and Wink, who was sitting on the fence watching, said I was squawking like a big crow. By the time he had jumped off the corral, I had got my knee out and turned her loose. I was fortunate to come out with only a stiff leg for a few days. The comical events

the colts stood in the corral hobbled this way with no saddle or bridle on them, you would jump up on their backs and start gentling them. They couldn't buck with the hobbles tied together, and even though they could jump around and sometimes would throw themselves, a young cowboy that was even halfway active shouldn't have too much trou-

The corrals on the Onyx Ranch where the boys broke the colts for the ranch in the 1930's.

that happened around those corrals at Onyx over the last one hundred years would fill several books.

After about a week of riding the first-year colts out of the corrals and down in the river bottoms, the colts were going pretty well. The Onyx Ranch crew of ten men were going up to Kelso Valley to help the Weldon boys gather their cattle. Wink decided to have me take my colts and go along. The Weldons were running about 200 head of mother cows south of Kelso Valley in the area around Mud Springs, Antimony Flat, and Pine Tree Canyon. The Weldon cattle usually ran on open range year round, but in 1948, because feed was short, they decided to move their whole herd to some leased land in Back and Sand Canyons. This was some fifteen miles to the west. Because the Weldon family range was adjoining the Onyx Ranch range in Kelso Valley, Rudnick and Alexander sent their crew to help.

As I was riding colts, I didn't play too big a part. Most of the days I just followed along as the crew gathered the wild bunch, and I mean they were wild! The three Weldon boys, Henry, Ray, and Sid, ran their cattle just as their dad before them had. They roped and branded the calves wherever they found them out on the range. Several times a year they would bring in all the three-year-old steers they could find to the home ranch where they had a

trap that made it a little easier to corral this kind of cattle. Sometimes they would have to leave a big steer tied to a tree for several days. Then, two men would go out and lead him back to the ranch, one with a rope on his head and one with a rope on one of the hind feet. After a couple of days watching a tree grow (with a short rope tied around his horns), his horns were pretty tender, and the steer would respond a little better than when he was first tied up.

I remember one day when I rode over the top of the ridge and looked down into Pine Tree Canyon. This canyon was mostly sage brush and Joshua trees with an oak tree or piñon pine scattered here and there. As I topped the ridge, I saw a scene that is hard to describe. The boys had jumped a small bunch of cattle, and they scattered like quail. They were able to hold a few of them together, but three or four just wouldn't be turned. There were cowboys going in every direction as they roped and tied these cattle. Some of the cows were twelve or thirteen years old and had never been in to the ranch.

We finally gathered only thirty-four head that day with a total of eighteen cowboys. As we were crossing Antimony Flat, a big ten-year-old bull quit the bunch and took off up the mountain. On one side, a cowboy by the name of Don Madson took off after him and roped him by the head just

Albert Burke, a South Fork cowboy.

118

before he reached the top of the ridge. This bull had never had a rope on him before or been taken to the home ranch. Don stopped the bull in a little swale that wasn't quite as steep as the rest of the mountain side. Ed Chappell, who wasn't far behind him, came in to try to catch the hind feet. Ed wasn't having much luck and Don was hollering that his honda was about to break. I spurred the sorrel mare I was riding up the mountain and got a rope on the bull's head just as Don's rope broke. We went around and around on the mountainside with Ed trying to get a rope on the bull's hind feet. The mare I was riding was in the bridle (a broke animal), but had a weak back and was almost laying her belly on the ground when the bull gave a good jerk. Don was tying a new honda and suggested I let the bull take off down the mountain to the flat where we had a better chance to handle him. I let him start down the mountain and was following him on the run when he went on one side of a juniper tree and my mare went on the other side. Because I had been riding colts, I didn't have much wrapping on my saddle horn. The smoke just flew as I went through the last three feet of my rope and lost it completely, without hardly slowing the bull down at all.

By this time, Don had finished building a new honda and had just completed running his rope through it while running his horse right alongside of mine. When I lost my rope, he rode up alongside the bull to try to turn him back towards the bunch while he was coiling up his rope to make another try at him. I was close behind him when I saw the bull whip his head around and rip an eighteen inch hole in the horse's belly. Although he almost lifted the horse off the ground, the horse kept running, still trying to turn the bull. As I watched in disbelief, I saw the entrails start to come out of this gaping hole and the horse was kicking them ahead with his hind feet as he ran with his ears back, still trying to turn the bull. Don hadn't realized how bad his horse was hurt until I hollered at him and told him. He pulled his horse up and stopped him. A couple of the boys roped the bull and we made a blindfold out of Dwight Pascoe's jumper and turned the bull in with the bunch. He was still pretty waspy, and when he heard the metal shoes of a horse in the rocks nearby, he would charge the sound. We knew we had to kill the horse as soon as possible and put him out of his misery, but nobody was packing a gun. I found a piece of pipe from an abandoned mine nearby, and after they stretched him out between two horses, I tried to kill him with

On the Onyx Ranch in the 1940's. From left: Wink Chappell, the cowboss; Art Alexander who, with his partner Oscar Rudnick, owned the ranch; and Glenn Alexander, who was in charge of farming and also helped work cattle at the ranch feed lot.

the pipe. I caved his head in, but still couldn't kill him. Finally, I had to cut his throat. Needless to say, not my favorite kind of work.

I was riding in the lead when we started down towards the Mud Springs field. The cattle were not far behind me when I got off and opened the gate. Just as I got back on my horse, an old cow came charging down the trail towards the gate. As I pulled my horse off to one side, I thought to myself, she sure is in a hurry to get into the field. However, I soon realized she wasn't going for the field, but was going for me! She chased me fifty yards up a steep bank. The mare was making big lunges up the hill. When I looked back, the cow was waving her horns right behind my mare's tail. The cow finally gave up and turned back into the field. This happened to me several times in the next few days. When you got a cow stopped, many times she would attack you with all the fury of a tiger.

There was one big steer on that range that was running loose with five ropes on him. He was so fast that he would outrun a horse after a man had roped him and the cowboy was forced to turn him loose. One evening, Wink Chappell rode into camp with five extra ropes. He said, "I got some ropes I'll sell to you boys for five dollars apiece." He was riding a horse that day called Redwing. He had roped the steer, thrown him, and tied him up a mile or so from camp. We went back the next day and led him in to the Weldon Ranch between two horses.

After we gathered the Weldon cattle, we took

Bev Robinson, Jr. when he cowboyed for the Onyx Ranch.

them to Walker Basin where the Weldons had rented some feed. Sometimes, when we were driving this wild bunch through brush country, Wink would have me in the lead singing (if you could call it that). This seemed to settle the cattle a little, as well as hold them back. There were men along both sides and everybody had to be on their toes to keep them together.

One Saturday, while the crew was in Walker's Basin, a few of us decided to go to Bakersfield and have some Chinese food at the Rice Bowl. We talked Wink Chappell into letting us borrow one of the ranch pickups and his last words were, "You guys remember we have to get up at four in the morning."

Four of us jammed into the front seat and took off. We had a good meal, but in the process of finishing it, someone remembered that there was a dance at Balance Rock that night. This meant a drive of two hours to the dance and a three hour drive to camp after the dance. We decided if we left when the dance was over at 1:00 a.m., with

Dwight Pascoe or Leonard Alexander driving (they were our fastest drivers), we could make it back to camp in time for breakfast. I don't remember what happened, but I do remember that we didn't make it back in time. I guess we figured we were fired anyway, so why not stay an extra day or two.

Monday night, we pulled into camp fully expecting to be fired. Wink was a good friend, and after giving us a good talking to, he warned us never to try that again. I thought we were pretty wild in those days!

All other accounts of cowboy fun in my early days seem to pale when put up beside the things the early vaqueros in California did for fun. When Zenas Leonard was out in California in 1833 with Captain Walker, he wrote the following account in his diary.* "On our way from the capital to our camp, we had an opportunity of witnessing a part of the Spanish mode of gambling in this country,

*Adventures of Zenas Leonard, Fur Trader, edited by John C. Ewers.

which was rare amusement to us, and which they call bull-baiting. It is in this fashion, as near as I could understand: when a number of sporting gentlemen get together for this purpose, they repair to the prairies, all well mounted and prepared for the chase. When they come across a herd of cattle, they make large bets on who shall be the first to noose one of the cattle in the drove in sight. When everything is arranged this far, they all take an even start. The one who gets the rope around the animal's horn or neck first claims the assistance of the rest to throw the animal to the ground, which ends the chase for this time. As the Spaniards are generally skilled in the art of throwing the noose, the chase in a case of this kind mostly depends on the fleetness of the horses.

"When they have secured a bull in this way, they take him to a pen made strong for this purpose, where they put him in for safe-keeping, then they settle the bets. Having got through with this game, to give the losers an opportunity to regain their losses, they start out on the hunt of a grizzly bear, always preferring the largest, which they capture in the same way. Taking a bear is a much more dangerous piece of work, than any other animal, owing to their enormous strength. It often happens that, in taking a bear, they are unhorsed; when, if alone, they are in imminent danger of being tore to pieces; but this seldom happens unless the horse is thrown, or the saddle tore loose.

"In taking a bear, their object is to noose him round one of the hind legs, in order to keep him from biting the cord, which they are very apt to do if fast round the neck. A single hunter can do but little with a large bear, and they are seldom attacked single handed, or without the certainty of assistance from some of their comrades. When overtaken by the foremost rider, the bear stops running and prepares for war. This man will then engage the attention of the bear by teasing him, whilst another hunter will come up in the rear of the excited animal and noose him by the hind foot; when the cord is securely fastened to the hind foot, he is generally considered safe. It is then that their sport begins in good earnest, and the feats that are sometimes performed by the men, bear, and horses would be incredible to any person who has never seen any sport of this kind.

"After the bear finds himself secure and has become pretty well worried, he seats himself sullenly on the ground and lets the horse pull at the cord, stretching his leg out until the pain becomes too severe, when he will draw up his leg, horse and all, with as much apparent ease as a horse would a sleigh. I have been told that some of the largest bears have been known to drag two horses a considerable distance in a fit of rage, in spite of all the exertions of the horses and riders to the contrary.

"After the bear is pretty well worried in this way, another noose is fastened round one of the fore feet

Onyx Ranch crew at the McGuick Place in 1948. From left: Johnny Sousa, Leonard Alexander, Ed Chappell, Dwight Pascoe, Bev Robinson, Jr., Wink Chappell, Henry Weldon, Loraine Smith Bailey and Bob Powers.

or neck, when the bear will commence beating the ground with his feet and manifesting the most intense rage and anger imaginable—and in this manner they drag, whip, and coax him along to the pen where the bull is confined.

"Their cords are made of green cowhide, which they cut into narrow strips, hang them in the sun, and rub them as they dry, making them soft and pliable, when they are plaited into a rope which no weight can sever.

"When the bear has arrived at the bull pen, their bets on taking him and all disputes are settled, refreshments taken, and preparations made for another scene, which is by far the most pleasing to the Spaniards. They begin to enrage the bull by pricking him with a nail fixed in the end of a stick, and when his anger has rose to the war pitch, the bear is let into the pen with the bull. The men now bet all they are worth on which will be the conqueror, and everything manifests the greatest possible excitement.

"Sometimes the animals refuse to fight until they are forced to it by being tormented with the sharpened sticks, but when one receives a blow from the other, nothing can part them until one or the other falls. These fights last sometimes half an hour without relaxation. The bear is much the strongest, but it has no chance of avoiding the thrusts of the bull, in consequence of the smallness of the pen; but in an open field, a grizzly bear will conquer a bull in a few moments.

"When the fight is over, the conquered animal is taken out and the bets are again settled. If it is the bear that is whipt, the game is continued and the bets renewed on some person who will offer to go into the pen with the enraged bull, lay his hand on some part of his body, and escape untouched. This is by far the most dangerous part of the whole play, and many lives have been lost at it; but so fond are the Spaniards of gambling, that in play a life is of but little consequence. When the bets are arranged, the adventurer stands at the door of the pen with his blanket in his hand, and the company is occupied in maddening the bull. When he has become sufficiently enraged, the hero steps in, when the bull will make a desperate plunge at him with his horns, which the man escapes by throwing the blanket over the face of the bull and blinding him—he then claps his hand on the designated spot, snatches the blanket off his horns and makes his escape. If he gets out without the bull striking him, he has won the stakes for all those who bet on him—which will

be a profitable business for him, as he receives a certain percentage on all the money thus won."

One day, while we were still working the Kelso Valley area, two big steers started down the canyon. Wink told me to see if I could take them on into the Weldon Ranch. We were about three miles from where there was a holding field that was fairly easy to run cattle into. The steers ran the whole three miles. They only tried to break off on the right side, and by staying off to the right a little, I was able to get them into the field. I was riding the colt called Skunk that day, and after running the three miles, Skunk was hardly breathing hard. His toughness was only topped by his meanness. Sometimes, when I was riding him, he would kick at one of my feet in the stirrups, whirl, and buck. And could he buck! I guess he was the only horse on the ranch that bucked Wink Chappell off. Several times he should have bucked me off. One time he had me bucked off about three times, then bucked back under me. He was dipping so low that twice my feet scraped the ground. He was giving me such punishment that I wished he had bucked me off. This happened coming from Dove Springs just before we got to Butterbredt Flat.

About two weeks later, I "staked out a claim" on Butterbredt Flat (that's what a cowboy called a spot where he was bucked off). I was riding a little sorrel mare we had raised on our home ranch and that I had ridden a hundred times. This time, I was riding my roping saddle and couldn't quite stay with her. When I was bucked off, I hung on to the hackamore rope and the reins of my spade bit. As I went off over one shoulder, I took the double reins with me and pulled her right over on top of me. I grabbed her head and held her down long enough to get my senses back and get loose from her. Besides landing on my backside, I skinned up my face pretty good on one side. As we were taking the cattle down Kelso Canyon towards the Mack Ranch, my dad came driving up the dirt road with Art Alexander. I had a bloody bandana wrapped around my head with just one eye showing through. I'll never forget how mad my dad was. He said I was trying to kill myself. That was one of the reasons he never wanted me to ride colts when I was growing up. He was always afraid I would get killed.

He should have remembered how he felt the time he told me about his grandmother, Sophia Smith, coming out to the corral at the Smith Ranch and making him get off a colt when he was a teenager. This was the same corral at Smith's where I got

Bob Palmer on his cattle range at Bonita Meadow.

Matt Burlando, a Kern River cattleman.

bucked off several times. There was a black mare the young cowboys used to try to ride on Sunday afternoon in the 1940's. The corral was hard as cement with rocks sticking up in it and an irrigation ditch running through one corner. We would snub the mare up to another horse, then get on with just a loose rope for a hand hold (instead of a bareback rig such as they use in a rodeo competition). One time when I was bucked off, I lit on the seat of my pants so hard I didn't realize I had also jammed my right arm into that hard ground and broken my wrist. We were eating dinner later that evening and Wink Chappell said, "Bob, what's wrong with your arm?" I said, "It sure is sore." He said, "I guess it is; see that hump? It's broken." Dumb cowboys!!

One time Leonard Alexander got bucked off in that same corral. The black mare bucked toward a gate and turned at the last minute, sending Leonard bouncing across the corral and ending up under the gate. Once Lyman Petersen pulled a dismount that didn't hurt much but his feelings. He was riding the same black mare, using my Brydon Brothers bronc saddle. I guess the saddle wasn't cinched tight enough. The old mare got her front legs up by her neck and bucked Lyman off, saddle and all, right in a foot of mud and water where the ditch ran through the corner of the corral. He sure looked funny sitting there in the water with his feet still in the stirrups.

Getting back to Butterbredt Flat, I think the time I got bucked off, I finished off my back, and brought about an end to my bronc riding days.

John McNally, a Kern River cattleman.

Cecil Pascoe, a top horse trainer, on Nugget.

I tried to ride, off and on, for the next six years, but my back hurt too much. In 1955, I had my first spinal fusion, then another in 1973. As much as I loved to ride colts, I didn't have the natural coordination it took to make a good bronc rider, but if I hadn't hurt my back, I think I would have stuck with it.

I quit the Onyx Ranch because of my back, and while I rode for several years, I didn't enjoy it too much because of the discomfort. We sold the ranch in 1952, and I didn't ride much for the next thirty years.

# The "New" Cattle Business

"A man never starts to learn until he discovers how little he knows." Of all the sayings heard on the ranches, the foregoing is the most quoted by those who really know cattle. By the time I came to this point, I was almost sixty years old and I realized that I wouldn't live long enough to be counted as either a top cowhand or an expert in managing a cow and calf outfit. However, because of my love for cowboying, the cow business, and those involved with it, I have attempted to pass on a small part of what I have learned.

The following two chapters may be of interest only to those who run cattle for a living, but I have included them with the hope that some of this information, while just one man's opinion, might be helpful.

After we sold the family ranch in 1952, my main contact over the next thirty years with my home range and families who ran cattle there was in connection with the various positions I held for the Forest Service while working in that area. My position for this agency when I retired was that of Range Officer. It was part of my job to check the high country meadows in the spring to determine when the feed was ready to allow several thousand head of cattle to come onto the forest for about three months of summer grazing. When the time was right, I would count the cattle onto the forest, and during the season check feed conditions to ascertain when they would be removed in the fall.

After my retirement from the U.S. Forest Service I worked on one of the local ranches. I held a job as manager on this ranch for five years during the early 1980's. I found that the cattle business had changed immensely over the intervening thirty years. It was a whole new ball game! The price of cattle had gone up about a third, but operating ex-

Bob Powers, cowboy and author.

penses had gone up at least 130%. Cattle ranching was getting to the point where you could no longer run your business the way your father and grandfather ran it, which was, in most cases, by tradition and emotion. Ranchers had to tighten up and make their cows produce more to pay for skyrocketing costs. The ranches that made these changes had a chance to make a living for their owners.

The cow and calf producers who didn't change either went broke and sold out, or the ranches were supported by outside income. In some cases, the income came from oil royalties or land sales, but as a greater number of ranchers failed to make a go of it, their ranches were bought up by doctors, lawyers, and people in other professions who used the ranch as a hobby, or in some cases, for tax deduction purposes. Some of these new owners of the cow and calf outfits hired competent, knowledgeable people to operate their ranches, using all the new technology available. Others, however, continued to let nature take its course by employing outdated practices such as raising their own bulls and being satisfied with a sixty percent calf crop of small, substandard calves.

The big advantage the cow and calf producer of the 1980's has over the one of the 1950's is the world of information available to put together an operation that makes sense, and also makes money. In fact, there is so much new information at a rancher's disposal that many are snowed under by the volume of it. You get advice from the university researcher, the veterinarian, banker, accountant, equipment salesman, and your lawyer. It is very true that conditions under which university experiments are carried out are hardly ever present on the ranch, but it at least gives you a place to start. If all this information doesn't confuse you and you want more information, you can take all the trade magazines, such as the *Beef* magazine and the *Livestock Digest.* You can go to all the cattlemen's conventions and not only listen to the experts, but also find a big supply of written information to read later. Some are so bombarded by the flood of information that after reading or hearing of fifty ways you might increase your profit in the cow and calf business (none of which would be applicable in your type of operation), you might let an idea or method slip by that would work ideally for you. The main thing to realize is that there is no magical solution. By sifting through the reams of information, you should be able to pull out bits and pieces here and there that would work for you. I know you would have to have a crystal ball to know for sure if a new idea would make you money by incorporating it into your operation, but by really knowing your operation, you should be able to avoid throwing money away on ideas that have no chance of working.

The most important ingredient in any type of cattle operation is your feed source. If yours is a cow and calf operation, in order to make everything else work right you have to have plenty of good, preferably inexpensive feed between the time your cows calve and when they are bred back. The rest of the year is important too, but this is the critical period. If you don't have a reliable source of feed at a reasonable price, it is almost impossible to make your operation pay, even if you do everything right.

According to those operators who have been successful, management plays a big part in the success or failure of your cattle business. You really have to keep your cost to a minimum. Very seldom will the profits from a cattle operation pay for new barns, facilities, or new four wheel drive pickups. Maintenance seems to be the key, not only on fences and windmills, but on equipment as well. When you do have to buy equipment, shop around and buy some good used equipment, or if you have to build new fences or corrals, build them to last the longest possible time.

M. E. Ensminger, in his fifth edition of his popular text, *Beef Cattle Science,* estimates that eighty to ninety percent of the progress realized in most beef herds comes about through the bulls used. There seems to be little doubt in the minds of most progressive beef breeders that proper bull selection is the most effective way to make genetic progress in a beef herd. If this is so, the cattleman's selection of his herd sires is one of the most important decisions. In making this decision, your first question would be what breed you would pick. Because there are over 30 breeds available, and all the crosses available from the combinations of these breeds, many cattlemen are in a dilemma to choose an appropriate breed. What breed or combination of breeds your cow herd is made up of will be one of your considerations. Also, the type of operation you are involved in is another thing to consider. Are your cattle on fenced pasture land a big part of the year, or are they on open range?

I think back to the breed of cattle we had on our ranch when we sold in 1952. For years we were allowed to put only registered Hereford bulls on the Fish Creek Allotment. In the early 1940's, my dad had purchased fifty head of heifers from Etta Andress that had a lot of Shorthorn blood. As they began to calve after being bred to the Hereford bulls, we were getting bigger calves and they also gained faster. What we didn't know at that time was that most of the improvement was due to what is known as heterosis, or hybrid vigor. This is a biological phenomenon which causes crossbreeds to outproduce the average of either of their parents. This has been used successfully for many years in many breeding programs. One example is the sheep business, where about eighty percent of all lambs marketed are crossbreeds. Swine and laying hens are, to a great degree, an example of the advantages realized from crossbreeding. It is estimated that ninety-five percent of all broilers sold are hybrids.

The genetic explanation for the hybrid's extra vigor is basically the same whether you are dealing with corn or cattle. Heterosis is produced by the fact that the dominant gene of one parent is usually more favorable than its recessive partner. When the genetic groups differ in the frequency of genes they have and dominance exists, then heterosis will be produced.

Hybrid vigor can be best explained by taking two herds of different breeding and switching bulls. If each herd had an average weaning weight of 400 pounds for all calves at 205 days, the average weaning weight from the crossing of these two herds could be expected to rise to 420 pounds. This would mean that the amount of heterosis was five percent or twenty pounds.

Not all traits show as much response to hybrid vigor. Traits that are high in heritability, such as tenderness of ribeye, show little response to hybrid vigor, but respond consistently to selection. On the other hand, traits low in heritability, such as mothering ability, conception rate, and calving interval, respond well to hybrid vigor.

Hybrid vigor in a cow herd will increase fertility, milk production, result in more calves surviving, calves growing at a faster rate, and by the cows giving you more years of service. These are all important traits because they mean more profit to the cattleman.

An important part of hybrid vigor depends on genetic difference between the two breeds crossed. In other words, crossing a Brahman and Hereford would result in more hybrid vigor than crossing two English breeds such as Herefored and Angus.

Again the question arises: what breed of bulls should a cattleman use? If you would ask this question of ten cattlemen, you might get the names of ten different breeds or a combination of any ten breeds. In most cases, the cattleman will base his answer on the type of cattle he has seen best adapted to his particular range and type of operation.

My personal preference of bulls would be the Simmental, Gelbvieh, or Beefmaster to breed to a herd of almost any kind. I think you would probably get a more noticeable gain in weaning weight, too, by using a three-breed-cross based on these breeds. Both the Simmental and Gelbvieh breeds have a history of high milk production and the Beefmaster, especially the Lasater Beefmaster, also have been bred for milk production. The cow-and-calf-man's main cash crop is his calves, and weaning weight in beef calves is influenced more by how much milk the mother gives than by any other single factor.

It has been estimated that most beef cows give only an average of ten pounds of milk per day. Ex-periments have proven that a calf that gets an extra gallon (8.6 pounds) of milk per day can be expected to be about 150 pounds heavier at weaning time. Because milk production in beef cows is about thirty-two percent heritable, infusion of a breed with heavy milking capabilities into a herd will raise the weaning weights of the calves in just a few generations. The three breeds I mentioned earlier are also all known for having exceptionally high daily gain records and good temperaments.

There are several ways to buy bulls, but the one that seems the most logical to me is to find a breeder in the same type of country that you run your cattle in. You can take cattle from a hard scrabble range in Mexico and they will do well almost anywhere, but take cattle raised in small pastures and they might not do well at all on a desert range. I would look for a breeder that had been in business for quite a few years and has sires from the top blood lines of that specific breed. You can check with the association for the breed that you are interested in and get sire summaries. From looking at the herd sires, if any have been on gain test, you can study these records. I feel it would be best to buy your bulls at an age from twelve to fourteen months of age. Using yearling bulls, you have to use more bulls, one bull to twenty cows for a sixty-five day breeding period. With more mature bulls, two years old and beyond, one bull will be sufficient for thirty cows for the same sixty-five day breeding period.

When going to a ranch to select yearling bulls, you will be picking from young bulls that were all born about the same time. You will be choosing the largest calves in the herd. You might want to throw out any individuals that had an exceptional high birth weight, anything over 110 pounds. A bull that has an exceptionally high birth weight will probably throw calves that are too big and apt to cause calving problems.

You will be looking for bulls that have a strong, straight top line, well-sprung foreribs, and also well muscled. When looking at the bull from the rear, the back and loin should be sloping gently downward. You will be looking for bulls that are long and tall, but not excessively fat. The bull should be deeper in the fore-flank than the rear flank. There should be a well defined groove down the top line. This will be caused from the rib-eye bulging on each side of the backbone. You should also be able to see the muscles when the animal walks.

How much can a cattleman afford to pay for a

127

good bull? In Ensminger's *Beef Cattle Science,* he states that in his opinion commercial cattlemen can afford to pay as much as $1,950 for a superior bull rather than pay $600 for an ordinary bull. He bases this on the asumption that calves sired by a superior bull will average twenty-five pounds more at weaning time. Assuming that twenty-five calves are weaned annually from cows bred to this bull, over the period of three years the bull is in service, at fifty cents per pound, that is an extra twelve dollars and fifty cents per calf or $312.50 per year, or $937.50 for the three years. In 1987, the price of these calves would be closer to sixty cents per pound; this could add another $250.00. Ensminger feels that this bull, because of his added size, will bring an extra one hundred dollars over the ordinary bull when sold for slaughter, bringing the total to $1,350.00 over what you would gain from the average bull. If the cattleman is raising his own replacement heifers, a further bonus will be accrued from the superior sire through his daughters.

If a bull breeder has one hundrd head of yearling bulls for sale and he lets you take the top cut, he would probably charge on a sliding scale of $1,600 for the top first ten picked. The last ten to sell would go for $1,000. These figures are purely theoretical. If you were picking from the same number of two-year-old bulls, you might expect to pay an extra two hundred dollars each.

Outside of bull selection, I think the next most important consideration with a beef herd would be calving percentages. A good many breeders settle for 85% calf crop, and that probably is hard to beat without using drastic measures. Most breeders save about 20% of their heifers for replacements, but with the method I'm advocating, you would save 80 to 90 percent of your heifers, culling only those that are smaller than usual or that have a small pelvic measurement. These measurements could be taken by a veterinarian. These measurements, plus age, weight, and the desired size of the calf, help to project calving ease. Even though this could cost at least $1.50 per heifer, it would probably be money well spent.

How old will your heifers be when they have their first calf? Although surveys indicate that at least 50 percent of heifers that calve as two-year-olds require help calving, and as many as fifteen percent of the calves and five percent of the heifers are lost, many ranchers still calve their heifers first at two years old instead of at three. One of the advantages is that over a heifer's lifetime you will have one more calf and an added calf weight of about 400 pounds. A cattleman's biggest success in calving out two-year-olds comes from using bulls on them known to sire small calves at birth. Cattlemen for quite a few years have been using Angus bulls that throw small calves; in recent years, Longhorn bulls have gained popularity. I have seen the best results using Jersey bulls. You rarely have to pull a half-Jersey calf even from a two-year-old. The resulting half-Jersey offspring may not please some cattlemen because of their "dairy cow" looks. However, a half-Jersey calf sold off the cow will probably bring only about thirty dollars less than one from a bull of the beef breeds. If I had beef cattle at this time, I would keep these half-Jersey heifers in my cow herd because of the extra milking ability, which will be handed down through the generations. They also have well-shaped udders and strong udder attachments. The fact that even a small amount of Jersey blood in a heifer or cow will give her the ability to calve more easily is also of supreme importance, especially if she might be calving on the open range where you can't watch her closely. If you are a cow and calf man, what you are selling is pounds of *live* calf.

For many cattlemen, having Jersey blood show in any of the cows in their cow herd would be as unacceptable as riding a plow horse out to cut cattle. I wouldn't mind seeing a little brindle stub-horned cow in my herd as long as she had a calf by her side that was almost as big as she was.

The heifers you save for replacement would be put with the bulls at thirteen to fifteen months of age. After a sixty-five day breeding season, the bulls are taken out. After waiting forty to sixty-five days and testing for pregnancy, the ones not bred should be sold. Your cow herd should have this same sixty-five day breeding season and also be pregnancy tested after the same waiting period. All cows not bred should be sold. If you also sell every cow who fails to wean a heavy calf, you should, after a few years, have a ninety-five percent calf crop.

It may not be realistic for some ranchers to try for a ninety-five percent calf crop, but the best chance any livestock producer has in achieving this goal is by being really hard-nosed in your culling. A cow might be ideal in disposition and conformation, but if she fails to have a large calf by her side at weaning time, she is just a liability and should be sold. By consistently demanding more from your cows, the highest possible goals should be realized.

Animal health should be a big consideration to those running a cow and calf business. Disease can cut into your profit as much as $100.00 per calf. Thirty years ago most ranchers only vaccinated for blackleg and malignant edema. However, today there is a raft of different diseases that most ranchers vaccinate for, not to mention internal and external parasites. Some experts feel that money spent on animal health will return to the cow and calf operator as much as $5.00 to $15.00 for each $1.00 spent. However, some dollars do not return one cent. You should examine those animal health dollars just as closely as any other dollar before they go out.

Each ranch needs to adopt a herd health program. This involves planning in advance so you can use modern technology to head off health problems that might siphon off profits.

While each ranch operation is unique and each year can bring new problems with a health program, many of these problems can be solved. Quite a few ranchers today start their calves at branding time with a vaccination program suited to their particular area.

The first step is to find a competent veterinarian and together work out a system of livestock health. These individuals have invested a vast amount of time and money in their chosen profession, and most keep current on changes in disease prevention in animals. If you find, as I did, in Dr. Ralph Walton of Tulare, California, a top flight veterinarian who is also a great cowboy, you are indeed fortunate.

To summarize what in my opinion should be an ideal cow and calf operation, would be one where I could run 500 to 1,000 head of cows. The feed would come at the right time of year so you could plan for fall calving (August and September). The cows would then be put in with the bulls in November for a forty-five to sixty-five day breeding period. Sixty days after the bulls are taken away from the cows, I would pregnancy-test my cows and sell all those not bred. In May and June I would wean my calves, which at this time should average 600

Gary Walker, on Hot Star Chex, working a cow at the 1983 Snaffle Bit Futurity at Reno, Nevada.

Jim Walker, a Tulare County cowboy with two of his favorite horses. Joker (left) and Evil Eye.

pounds. I would either sell my steer calves right off the cows or at least retain part ownership through a feedlot. Owning the proper type of cattle, after 160 days in the feedlot, these steers would weigh 1,100 pounds and grade 80% choice when butchered. The heifers, after being culled mainly for small pelvic measurement, would be put with the Jersey bulls in November for the same sixty-five day breeding period as the cows. Those not with calf after this period would be sold.

Using this plan, your cull cows and heifers could be sold after March, when the prices are good and your steer calves would also be ready for sale in May and June while prices are still generally high.

Although I know the above is only a hypothetical situation, how I would love to have the chance to see how it would work!

Herb Young, Kern River cattleman, at the Kennedy Meadow branding for the Alexander Ranch in 1987.

130

# COLOR PORTFOLIO

Longhorn cows owned by Larry and Sandra Southard. Sandra is a great granddaughter of Billie Boen. Note the various colors.

A longhorn cow owned by the Southards. Her coloring is typical of the coloring of cattle that were found on the coast of California during the 1830's.

John Wofford rides his high country range with his grandson John Perkins and his niece Michelle Robinson.

L to R, Steve Perkins and Tom Costa, two Wofford Ranch cowboys on the porch of the Bonita cabin in the High Sierras.

Herb Queen, a Poso Creek cattleman.

The old Powers' house, a mile west of Onyx, that Marvin and Isabel lived in for thirty years. Each one of their three sons started married life in this same house. In 1987 all that was left was the little brick storehouse on the right.

Bill Horst keeps the cattle moving past Big Pine Meadow. This meadow was homesteaded by Marvin Powers, Sr. in 1919.

Bill and Bob Powers in 1946.

Cowboys on the Alexander Ranch. From left: Walter Mecham on Cho Cho, Bob Powers on Pal, and Butch Behm on Bunny.

133

Taken at a cowboy barbecue on the South Fork in 1987. From left in back: Buzzy Palmer, Sylvia Hafenfeld, Ray Weldon, Roberta Joughin, Ken Rhoads, Leonard Alexander, Clifford Cross, John Nicoll, Dan Dennison, Bill Kissack, Herb Young, Bud Silicz, John McNally, Glenn Alexander, Dutch Henderson, Wynona Tipton, Tiese Quinn, Sis Staats, Tip Tipton, Sr., Marge Albitre, Jim Andreas, Sid Weldon, Lois Vig, Windy Chappell. In front from left: Marvin Powers, Jr., Bruce Hafenfeld, Gary Behm, Ed Chappell, Norvan Powers, Butch Behm, Ken Vineyard, Buckshot Tipton, Dale Creighton, Tippy Tipton, Jr., Buddy Montes, Richard Staats, and Bob Powers.

Cattle from the Fish Creek allotment graze just south of the Monache drift fence. North of this fence is the Monache Meadow allotment, also the boundary of the Inyo National Forest. Since this drift fence was built in 1913 it has been the boundary between the Inyo Forest and the Sequoia Forest. Olanche Peak is the sharp peak in the background. An early fall storm had painted these mountains white just two days before. The elevation is 8,000, and it was almost time to take the cattle back to the valley floor for the winter.

A bunch of cows trail down through Hooker Meadow as they leave the mountains in the fall. The quaking aspen leaves have turned to gold and most of the cattle are more than ready to leave.

The leaders of one of the cattle drives as they leave the mountains in the fall. These leaders have almost reached Big Pine Pass. The Fish Creek Range is just behind the second ridge, and in the far background you can see the snowy peaks of the Mt. Whitney Range.

In the foreground a couple of two year-old heifers and their half Jersey calves. The mother of the third calf is behind the Simmental bull. Next year these first calf heifers will have calves from the bigger bulls, such as Simmental or Gelbvieh.

One of the good Gelbvieh bulls on the Mojave Desert range.

Dale Creighton rides through some of his cattle on the edge of his spring range. Dale, a fifth generation rancher in the Kern River Valley, demands the most of his cattle, his land, and himself. He is considered by many to be one of the most progressive ranchers and farmers in Kern County. Dale is helped in his ranching operation by his wife, Debbie, and their six children.

Some of Dale Creighton's cows on the spring range. One of his best cows is on the left with her heifer calf out of a Simmental bull.

In the foreground, one of Dale Creighton's Simmental cross bull calves, in the back, a Brahman cross calf and his mother.

Bob Powers checks the cattle the modern way on Snake Creek Meadow in the high country. (Photo by Casey Christie.)

Looking down into the Dome Land Wilderness from the Sherman Pass Road. The South Fork of the Kern River runs just behind the rock domes.

Dr. Ralph Walton drags a calf to the branding fire at the Alexander Ranch branding.

Bob Powers with two of his cowboy friends, Dr. Ralph Walton (center) and Gary Walker (right).

Ralph Walton, Sr. and his Rocking R brand at a calf branding on his ranch.

Cattle come in to water at the windmill at Walker Well on the Walker Pass Allotment.

Cows come in to water at Big Spring overlooking the Mojave Desert.

The right weather condition brings an abundance of forb species. Many of these we think of as wild flowers. Whatever we call them, they furnish a super feed source.

Cows resting in the joshua trees during the heat of the day.

Because of the increased traffic and higher speeds on Kern County roads, more cattle are killed on the highway each year.

A good feed year on the Mojave Desert range in the 1980's.

# The Mojave Desert.. A Renewable Resource

Ranchers from the South Fork of the Kern River have been using areas of the Mojave Desert for 110 years. When Bill Landers moved his cattle on the Mojave in 1878, this land was under the jurisdiction of the Department of the Interior, which had been established in 1849 as part of the General Land Office created in 1812. The Department of the Interior was set up to establish controls on public lands, but being understaffed and not having clear guidelines, it was a long way from meeting its goals. In 1897 the Forest Preserves were established to be managed by the Department of the Interior. In 1898, Gifford Pinchot was appointed Chief of the Division of Forestry. Grazing policies were a major concern for Pinchot and his field agents. Studies and reports on the grazing issue were piling high on his desk. Grazing affected fire control, natural regeneration of the forest, soil productivity, and water supplies.

Pinchot's first move was to prohibit grazing in California forests, which included part of the Mojave Desert. Pinchot then hired Albert Potter, an Arizona range man, as chief consultant. By working with the stockmen, he brought order out of grazing chaos. In 1893, President Benjamin Harrison had created the six million acre Sierra Forest Reserve, the southern portion of which included the area of the Mojave we are concerned with (first called the South West Division). In 1900, the Department of Interior started hiring rangers to work in the field. In most cases, local men were hired. My grandfather, James H. Powers, was one of these. He started to work for the Department of Interior in 1900 and continued through June of 1902. Powers, a rancher himself, worked out of his home ranch or out of the ranch of Thomas H. Smith, his father-in-law. The following entry in his diary is typical of his activities: "March 21, 1902 - Left Smiths at 8 a.m. and traveled on road via Onyx to John McCray's place, then to John Nicoll's, then to W.W. Landers, and returned to Smiths arrived 4 p.m. Miles traveled 24." In areas of the Reserve that showed over-grazing by cattle, he took steps to correct the problem. He noted: "Brown's cattle to be cut by 75 head from original number. R. Neil's cattle to be cut 75, and Scodie cattle cut 50 head." While conditions were slowly improving, even up into the early 1930's, many problems such as over-grazing were still apparent.

James H. Powers, early South Fork cattleman.

In June of 1934, the Taylor Grazing Act was approved by Congress, and on September 12, 1934, President Roosevelt appointed Farmington R. Carpenter as the first Director of the Division of Grazing, which was later to become the Grazing Service.

Carpenter, a rancher and attorney from northwestern Colorado, didn't regulate from an office. He came into the field and got a first-hand opinion of what the conditions were. Carpenter stayed at the Onyx Ranch for two weeks and Windy Chappell was appointed by Rudnick and Alexander to show him the range. Because of men like Carpenter working with the stockmen, they were able to grasp the potential under the law and agreed to give it a try. On July 16, 1946, the General Land Office that was started in 1812, and the Grazing Service set up in 1934, were merged to form the Bureau of Land Management (B.L.M.).

Carpenter held the first meeting for the new Grazing Service in Bakersfield on January 18, 1935. Local cattlemen and sheepmen set up separate grazing areas on the Mojave Desert for sheep and cattle. A.J. Alexander of the Onyx Ranch attended his first meeting and helped establish the Mojave Grazing District. This was one of the first grazing districts in California.

In the early years, the public domain lands were considered to be of prime use for only mining and grazing of livestock, but after the B.L.M. was set up, the agency hired specialists that were trained in geology, soils, wildlife, range conservation, and recreation. In 1964, the Classification and Multiple Use Act was mandated for the administration of public lands for "outdoor recreation, range, timber, watershed, wildlife, and fish purposes."

What is this rangeland we are talking about? Of the 2.2 billion acres in the United States, only about fifteen percent is suitable for the production of crops. However about half of the land that will not grow crops does grow forage usable by livestock. The rest is made up of cities, roads, dense forest or other lands too steep or rocky to grow grass or browse. So the Mojave Desert Range is part of nearly a billion acres of range and pasture resource that can be used by food animals such as sheep and cattle. These are ruminant animals that are able to break down the cellulose in grass and other roughages.

Of the two types of digestive systems in large animals, the most common is the simple or Mongastric stomach. Those who contain this type of

stomach are man, swine, rats, cats, and dogs. The horse has only a simple stomach, but is able to utilize roughage because part of his large intestine, called the cecum, works as a fermentation vat, which operates like a cow's rumen.

Most of the animals with simple stomachs eat food that could also be eaten by man. This is because their daily amino acid requirements must be met by the protein they eat. Not only do they require protein, but the protein must be of high quality so they have all the essential amino acids. Bacteria in the rumen of ruminant animals digest the protein and use it to form new protein. The ruminant then digests the bacteria. Thus the type of protein a ruminant eats is not as important as the total amount of nitrogen in the diet.

Ruminant animals, such as cows, sheep, goats, deer, and buffalo, have four stomachs and are able to grow and thrive on food that is unsuitable for man.

The energy from the sun is converted by plants into chemical energy, and the energy that isn't needed for their own functioning is stored in the plants as either cellulose or starch. Cellulose, the most abundant component of plants, is therefore the most renewable organic product on this earth. This vast food supply, raised on the range, is probably the most energy-efficient aspect of agriculture. Agriculture, as a whole, takes advantage of only about three percent of the total energy used in the United States, and of this, less than five percent is consumed for beef production. This means that beef production only uses about .0015 percent of the total energy used in the United States. The biggest share of the energy used in livestock production is to grow feed grains and hay. Because most of the beef animal's life is spent on pasture or range where it harvests its own feed, the energy expended is fairly small.

As mechanical energy costs continue to go up, a food source like beef, where the main energy used is solar energy, will be even more important.

Cattle on the open range can be compared to a work force of huge proportions that works twenty-four hours a day, seven days a week, converting raw material into a finished product.

We could take, for instance, one portion of the Walker Pass Common Allotment administered by the Bureau of Land Management. It stretches along both sides of Highway 178 for approximately twenty miles from upper Canebrake on the west to Highway 14 on the east. It is comprised of approximately 35,000 acres. The elevations range from 3,000 to 8,500 feet, and the average annual precipitation is six inches at the lower elevation with increasing amounts at higher elevations. Snow is common on the high peaks. Temperatures range from below 20° Fahrenheit in the winter to over 100° Fahrenheit in the summer.

The perennial forage species provide the most consistent feed source year after year. This perennial forage includes both shrubs and grasses. There are numerous perennial shrubs on this allotment. The most important species for livestock are: Four-wing Saltbush (*Atriplex canescens*), Winterfat (*Ceratoides lanata*), Spiny-hop (*Grayia spinosa*), and the Desert bitterbrush (*Purshia glandulosa*). These shrubs are the main feed source for cattle in the winter. Four important perennial grass species are: Indian ricegrass (*Oryzopsis hymenoides*), Pine bluegrass (*Poa scabrella*), Squirrel-tail (*Sitanion hystrix*), and Desert needlegrass (*Stipa speciosa*). Also used to a lesser degree are: Bursage (*Ambrosia dumosia*), Shadscale (*Atriplex confertifolia*), Cattle spinach (*Atriplex polycarpa*), Nevada tea (*Ephedra nevadensis*), Green tea (*Ephedra viridus*), California buckwheat (*Eriogonum fasciculatum*), Desert aster (*Machearanthera tortifolia*), Thornbush (*Lycium spp.*), and Purple sage (*Salvia dorrii*). In addition, there is a perennial forb called Desert mallow (*Sphaeralcea ambigus*).

During the months of December and January, the feed provided by the perennial shrubs and grasses is dried material left from the previous year. The early rain softens this feed and makes it more palatable and also some regrowth will occur if the rains are spaced right and the temperature stays warm. In the spring and summer, most of the feed furnished by the perennial species is on the soft new growth.

If the year is a poor feed year because of lack of rainfall, low temperatures or excess wind, the bulk of the feed is from the above mentioned perennials and it takes an average of fourteen acres to furnish feed for one cow for one month. If all the conditions are right and you get a good feed year, the ephemeral feed production (such as wildflowers) will far exceed the perennial forage; the Bureau of Land Management will give authorization to increase the use. The ephemeral authorization may be issued when the ephemeral production exceeds 200 pounds per acre and the minimum of 200 pounds per acre production must be maintained through the growing season. On a good year, it takes only about eight acres to provide feed for each A.U.M. (Animal Unit Month or one cow for one month).

If the storms come right, the ephemeral feed can start in the fall and continue through the spring. There are only three ephemeral or annual grasses that are of importance for livestock on the allotment. These are: Cheat grass (*Bromus tectorum*), Red broome (*Bromus rubins*), and Schismus (*Schisus arbicus*). However, over one hundred annual forb species occur on this range. These forbs, many of which we think of as wild flowers, make spectacular displays when the conditions are right. Less than ten species of forbs are considered important for livestock. Among these are Coreopsis (*Coreopsis bigelovii*), Phacelia (*Phacelia fremontii* and *Tanacetifioia*), Fiddleneck (*Amsenckia tessellata*), Desert dandelion (*Malcothrix californica*), and Filaree (*Erodium circutarium*). Several of these forbs not only make good forage in green or growing stages, but also cure well and provide excellent forage after they stop growing and dry. Some of the open flats on the west of the range that have a lot of filaree are rated as high as five acres per A.U.M.

Many old desert cows have certain areas they head for when you turn them loose on the desert range in December. As the year progresses, they move to other areas. For instance, the first two months they are turned out, the main feed source is from perennial shrubs and grasses. If the cows are first turned out on the east side of the range they converge on the area around Razor Well and Walker Well, where there are Four-wing saltbrush and Winterfat. If they are first turned out on the west side of Walker Pass, the Desert bitterbrush and Desert needlegrass furnish the early feed.

The frequency of rain, wind, and warm days make the difference between the feed being just adequate or a bumper feed year. With a bumper feed year, the range will take care of more than twice the normal number of cattle.

The trouble was that a bumper crop didn't come often enough. Because of this, the Bureau of Land Management had to find ways of getting more grazing on normal and dry years. The most critical time for any range is during the first part of the growing season. It was discovered that the cattle should be kept off the range during this period at least every other year. This means, instead of one big pasture, you have to make a number of smaller pastures by using cross fences.

Controlled grazing has improved not only on

government grazing land but private pastures as well. The concept of controlled grazing of livestock was first introduced by Gus Hormay in the 1930's. Using what he called the Rest-Rotation Grazing System. Each year more information has been made available to the rancher.

There are seven major options to consider when developing a workable grazing system. These are: (1) control grazing frequency (includes complete rest), (2) control of livestock stocking rates, (3) control of livestock distribution, (4) control of timing (season of forage use), (5) control livestock kind and class, (6) control of forage utilization, (7) add artificial rehabilitation to the grazing strategy. There are about seventeen different grazing plans that can be used, but even after a plan is decided on it might have to be changed the next year as conditions change.

A certain portion of each dollar received from the ranchers for their grazing permits goes into what is called the Section Three Range Improvement Fund. The money from this can be applied for and used for range improvement projects. Cross fencing and water development projects are two projects that the ranchers can receive financial help on. Besides fencing, placement of water on the range is another way you can get cattle to graze where you want them to. If you let the cattle go wherever they want to over a large range, they overgraze some areas while other areas get no use.

It isn't as easy to implement controlled grazing on desert land, such as the Walker Pass Common Allotment, as it would be on improved irrigated pasture. However, by cross fencing and making water available in more locations, you can vastly improve the range. By controlling where the cattle graze, you can alternate your pastures each year during the growing season (January 1 to March 15) so they won't be grazed every year during this critical growing period.

A good example of an allotment that is being currently improved by grazing practices is the Rudnick Common Allotment. This allotment is directly south of the Walker Pass Allotment and includes 153,000 acres of government land combined with 167,000 acres of private land owned by the Rudnick Trust. This allotment, operated by Richard Rudnick, is part of the range that Bill Landers ran his cattle on in the last part of the 19th century.

Rudnick runs stocker cattle (cattle from one to two years old). Most of the 4,000 head Rudnick ships in annually are steers. Over thirty miles of

Richard Rudnick, the third generation to run cattle on the Onyx Ranch.

fence were built on the allotment during 1986. By using natural barriers, such as steep ridges and gullies which the cattle can't cross, plus a minimum amount of fencing, the 153,000 acre allotment is being cut up into twelve pastures.

By closely monitoring these pastures the B.L.M. and Rudnick will decide each year which pastures will be used and the period of use.

Rudnick is currently working with leading members of the National Audubon Society to further utilize some of the natural springs on his allotment. These springs which were developed for cattle grazing are the chief source of water for song birds and numerous species of upland game birds. The plan includes fencing a separate area for these birds.

Twice during my life I have taken pack trips up through the Golden Trout Wilderness area. As I traveled north into the Sequoia Park into areas where livestock grazing had been prohibited for years, I started to notice a marked change in the vegetation, especially in the meadows. The deer were just not taking enough of the growth, and after a few years, many of the grass species died out.

In the early 1950's, Allen Savory devised the Savory Grazing Method, and this unconventional

The Onyx Ranch crew that work the cattle on the Rudnick allotment. From left: Tip Tipton, Sr., Tippy Tipton, Wynona Tipton, Buckshot Tipton and Buddy Montes. (Photo by Casey Christie.)

approach has revolutionized grazing practices for many ranchers who have utilized it. Savory was a game ranger in Zimbabwe (formerly Rhodesia). Despite the presence of animal herds that numbered in the thousands, the range was lush and productive. (This was common to what the pioneers found when they came west in America, although there were vast herds of buffalo and antelope grazing on the lush pastures.) Savory found the same conditions in Africa, and finally realized the range was in such good condition because the herds were constantly on the move and this way the plants were given time to recover before the animals returned to them.

This observation helped him to develop what came to be known as the Savory Grazing Method (S.G.M.). This concept of controlled grazing has done more to increase the profit cattlemen can realize from their pasture resource, than any other one thing.

With this method, animals are moved at the rate that the plants are growing.

In the May 20, 1985 issue of the Livestock Mar-

ket Digest, there was published an interview with Mr. Savory. One of the questions asked him was, "If some people had their way they would eliminate cattle on public lands all together. Can you give us an example where this might be detrimental?"

His answer was, "A good example is found in the many protected plots installed in brittle environments throughout the U.S. in the 1930's to prove that removal of livestock would result in improvement of the land. With animals removed, there was indeed an improvement which apparently substantiated the view of conventional range science. However, the effects of the whole eco-system were not studied for sufficient time or in adequate depth. All that was being seen was the initial impact of stopping the overgrazing, combined with the residual beneficial effect of the impact the animals had created while still on the land. Once the residual effect of this animal impact wore off, the communities in the plots started to deteriorate. Plants died prematurely due to the lack of grazing or trampling. Soil surfaces were exposed and other adverse reactions set in. Today, where they can still

147

be found, these sites are visibly poorer than the surrounding unmanaged land subjected to periodic animal impact.

"The Chaco Canyon National Monument is a good example. For those unacquainted with it, this national monument has now been 'protected' from any livestock grazing on it for fifty years. The result to be seen today is that most of the grassland communities have died out. The area is characterized by much bare, eroding ground with deep gullies still actively cutting and endangering the ancient ruins it was set aside to protect. In fact, it is a good example that the lack of adequate animal impact is a greater cause of desertification in such environments than is overgrazing. The neighboring overgrazed tribal lands have not desertified nearly as badly in the same time with the same weather."

Mr. Savory was also asked the question, "What is animal impact?" His answer was, "Animal impact is hoof action, and other effects of large concentrations of animals, that churns the soil, increases ground litter and helps encourage seedling establishment. Animal impact is what tends to give us more plants per unit area.

"We have discovered that there are two basic environment types that we need to be aware of. At their extremes, we have named them 'brittle' and 'non-brittle' environments. Between the two extremes all gradations can be found. Brittle environments tend to have erratic growing seasons. What we did not realize was that although one donkey walking down a hill every day of the year will cause an eroding path by the end of the year, 365 donkeys doing the same thing for one day of the year do not produce the same result. Where one cow grazing a plant, day after day, damages and kills it, the same plant will benefit if one cow grazes it (while a thousand other cows stand around) and then leaves it until it recovers. The plant is thus not overgrazed. In fact, it benefits from the complex interrelationships set up by the animal's impact on the whole community."

The rancher can also see other things in the ecosystem getting out of balance, such as coyotes and lions. Before man started to interfere with nature, before there were any roads in the back country, the hunting pressure was minimal. The deer population was high enough that even though a male lion would kill a deer every third day, there were enough deer that it didn't make that much difference. The predator was doing what he was created to do, live on game such as deer. However, as more roads were put into the high country where the does raised their young, the deer herd started to decline. Hunting pressure further compounded the problem until in some areas there weren't enough available deer to feed the lion population, so they started killing cattle.

One person's answer to this was, "In all my years in the forest, I have only seen one lion and I have seen a lot of cows. It looks like you could afford to lose a cow now and then." Ask the small cattleman like Tippy Tipton or Frank Liebel. One year lions took almost their total calf crop in two separate canyons, twenty miles apart. Not calves they needed to make a profit, but calves that they hoped would help them break even for that year.

In my book, *North Fork Country,* I have included a chapter entitled "Mountain Men," which is a real eye-opener on the impact the lions make on the deer population.

The ranchers do contribute a lot to the open range. Along the twenty-mile stretch of range along highway 178 there are four windmills that furnish ninety-five percent of the water. This water is used by wildlife and range animals alike. Each year the rancher is out a considerable expense to maintain these windmills and watering troughs.

The ideal pasture is one that is in a location where twenty to thirty inches of rain falls a year, instead of the six inches that is normal on the Walker Pass Allotment. On the other side of the spectrum is in a locality such as Hawaii. Allen Savory reported the following in the August 19, 1986 issue of the Livestock Market Digest: "In Hawaii, the Kahua Ranch has implemented the Savory Grazing Method on planted pastures that normally are fertilized at great expense. Since implementing SGM in the last year, however, they have done away with fertilizing, increased their stocking rate by 215% and their weight gains on steers by 62%. Where before they could expect to produce 250 pounds of beef per acre, this year they produced 719 pounds per acre. What makes these figures startling is that the ranch suffered through five months of drought! And, despite the drought, there was a marked improvement in the condition of the pastures. The ranch was able to repay its capital costs of construction on the cell within seven months. The animals were finished one hundred days sooner and thus labor and fixed costs per head were reduced. The reduced per head cost led to a substantial increase in profitability. Net income for the cell jumped from $3,915 up to $51,943 per year, an increase of over $48,000. That produced a phenomenal 1300% increase in profitability in a single year."

Not everyone gets results like these. The key to the success on the Kahua Ranch, says Savory, "Is due to the exceptional management they have."

Mr. Savory imported the wagon-wheel shaped grazing cell. Although very few are actually shaped like a wagon wheel, the basic concept is to have water and corrals in the center and rotate your stock about every three days, or often enough that they won't go back and graze before the pasture is ready. You need enough grazing area to allow pasture to grow back anywhere from twenty to thirty days.

Records must be kept on how many times and for how long each paddock was grazed, along with comments on quality, growth rate, and production of forage. Livestock are not rotated from paddock to paddock on a one-two-three basis, but moved to the paddock that needs to be grazed next.

There is no such thing as a typical two hundred acre pasture, but in a 20-inch to 30-inch rainfall area, it should be possible to run three hundred cows in the thirty-paddock controlled grazing layout for most of the year. The approximately $4,000 worth of fencing results in a total one-time cost of $13 per head.

Assuming we produce 253 weaned calves (85 percent weaning percentage) that average 500 pounds each, that works out to 127,500 pounds of beef, or 637.5 pounds per acre. On a fifty cent calf market, our gross profit would be $318.75 per acre—without tractor or fuel; little or no fertilizer, herbicides or irrigation, a minimum amount of labor and a maximum of satisfaction.

Excellent material on resource management can be obtained by contacting the Center for Holistic Resource Management, P.O. Box 7128, Albuquerque, New Mexico 87194. This center was formed as a non-profit foundation by Allan Savory and a group of concerned ranchers. The Savory Letter and a course catalogue listing courses held through the year in the Western United States is also available by contacting the center.

This author, along with Savory, and many others, is convinced that controlled grazing will predominate in years to come in the "new" cattle industry. It is natural to resent or be suspicious of anything new, and it would be so much easier for cattlemen to just go on running cattle like they did thirty years ago. However, many have found they must change if they are going to survive in the cattle business.

The "good stuff" is riding out on the Mojave Desert on a fresh spring morning with the perfume of acres of purple sage in your nostrils, to see the bunches of new-born calves that have been left with one of the mother cows to baby-sit while the rest of the mothers are off feeding or going to water; to ride the lush high country meadows in the summer to check on your herd; or bringing them out in the fall to sell the calves; then returning in January to the desert to start the cycle all over again.

I think one of the things that I have always enjoyed the most about ranch work, especially the cattle end, is you never know when you go out in the morning what the work that day will entail. Take one day, for instance, when Walt Mecham and I had taken a stock truck up to Kennedy Meadows to bring out a few head we had missed on the fall drive. There had been a little snow storm the week before, so instead of using the Chimney Peak Road, we went from the home ranch at Weldon to Kennedy Meadows by way of the Mojave Desert, going east on Highway 178, then north up the desert on Highway 14 to Nine Mile Canyon, and then to Sacatar Meadows in Kennedy Meadows.

We located the five head we were looking for, and with no trouble, loaded them at the loading chute in the stock truck. We then tied the stirrups up on our saddles, took the bridles off, and ran our horses in with the cattle. We started back down Nine Mile with Walt driving and me riding shotgun. The road down Nine Mile Canyon drops about 2,000 feet in eight miles and in most places is cut in the rocky, sandy hillside that falls off about half a mile to the creek bottom. In most cases the slope the road is built on is about forty percent downgrade. The canyon dropped off on my side to the creek. As usual, I was watching out the window for cattle. Although it wasn't our range, there was always a chance that a few cattle might work their way into this canyon. (It really doesn't matter if I'm close to my home range or not, or if my wife and I are driving to the coast, or even if we are in Hawaii, I am always watching for herds of beef cattle along the way. I especially like to see them on open range. I note the breed, what shape they are in, and what kind of feed they are on.)

As we proceeded about half way down Nine Mile Canyon, I caught a glimpse of some animals in some willow trees at the bottom of the canyon. I told Walt to stop and we got out to take a closer

**Walt Mecham bringing cattle out of the high country. A good cow-hand, a good friend.**

look. I took the binoculars I had in the truck and started looking them over. At first, I couldn't tell if they belonged to the ranch or not, but after we had stopped several minutes, they started getting nervous and milling around in the brush. With only about 300 head of grown cows on the ranch, I could recognize most of them even at some distance.

The first one I spotted that I knew belonged to our brand. She was a light red cow with a big red spot on her forehead the shape of a triangle, and horns that turned in. She was one of the few I always watched real close if I was on foot in the corral with her, as she would just as soon run over you as around you.

The next one that worked out in the open was a cow we call the giraffe. She was a big red and white spotted cow that is a natural poll (no horns). Whatever genes run in her blood are very strong, because regardless of the bull she is bred to, her calves always have the same markings and are al-

ways polls. Most of the bulls on the ranch are horned bulls that have been dehorned as calves.

There was an old corral and loading chute right close to the road about three and one half miles down the canyon, so I told Walt I would try to work them on down. Our horses had worked their way to the back of the truck, so we backed into the bank and let down the tailgate and let my horse out. It took some fast moves to get my horse out and the back ramp up before the five head of cows in the truck realized what was happening, or they would have boiled out over the top of us. Walt was to take the truck on down to the corral and unload his horse so he could help me corral and load the bunch we had spotted.

About six weeks earlier, I had ridden among these same cows almost every day and they would hardly pay any attention to me except maybe to keep a close watch on my dog, Tippy. After not seeing anyone for a month or so, they get wild real

**150**

fast. The only difference between the way they acted and the action of real wild cattle is that these cattle, after they are stopped and held up a few minutes, get gentle quickly, whereas those from the wild bunch of cattle who have been out for a year or two and escape several roundups, usually remain wild even after they are brought back to the ranch. These animals customarily have to be sold, as they just make others in the herd wild.

I started riding back up the road to give them the idea I wasn't after them, and when I was up the road about a half mile, I would cut into the canyon above them. The horse I was riding was named Cho Cho. He had been given this name because when we bought him he was windbroken. This was caused from someone running him too hard for too long. Otherwise, he wasn't too bad a horse. He just couldn't make those long runs, because after you ran him just a short distance, he would huff and puff for an hour. When I thought I was far enough above the cattle, I started off the hill, cutting a wide circle above them. From the way they started to

mill around nervously, I figured I might have a run. I wanted to take them down canyon to the corral so we could load them, and I was trying to ride around them far enough that if they made a break to go up the canyon, I would still have a chance to head them off on a horse that couldn't run too far. In a case such as this, you always have to expect the unexpected. In other words, local cattle or cattle used to running in this particular canyon would high-tail it down canyon if they got spooked because they would have a better chance of getting away.

I was about three-fourths of the way around to where I could head them down-country when they took off on the run—the wrong way. By pushing my horse pretty hard, I was able to make a short run and turn them. If there had been two of us horseback, one would have slipped down the canyon while they were occupied with their run up-canyon. That way, we could have controlled them better with one in front and one in back. They could not go up either side, as it was too steep. Walt had to get the corral ready, so I had to do it by myself. When I

Bob Powers brings a herd of cows and calves from the summer range to the home ranch.

turned them, I just sat there until they were out of sight down the canyon. I know they were looking back to see if I was on their tail, but I hoped by giving them lots of air, they might get some of the run out of their systems. The horse was already winded, but I hit a slow trot so they wouldn't get too far ahead of me. When I got close to where they went out of sight, I slowed my horse to a walk and kind of sneaked over the rim of the hill. They had stopped about a quarter of a mile away and were looking back. They started off on a fast trot when they saw me. Again, I let them get out of sight. They were following an old road along the creek bottom and couldn't go much of any way but down. Before long, they were starting to tire a little so I could keep in sight of them, but I tried to keep them from feeling crowded. When they went out of sight, I would trot a little to work up closer to them. The canyon was starting to widen and they had more chance of slipping away. I was watching them as close as I could from that distance. I came over a rise in the old road and didn't see them ahead where they should have been, so right away I knew they were trying to give me the slip. The creek bottom was off to my right a ways and I ran my horse the two or three hundred yards over where I could see in among the trees and willows. I just barely got ahead of them as they were heading back up the canyon. They were on the run again and started out of the canyon on the side about where I wanted them. This was the side the corral was on and easier going, as the main canyon from here on down was really rough. All of a sudden they disappeared in a draw. I could see they hadn't continued up, so I figured if they wanted to take the hard way down, I would let them. They had just crossed under the Los Angeles Water and Power Aqueduct, which turned sharply up hill on the right side of the canyon.

By this time, I guess they thought if they were going to be hassled they would start for their home range (winter range), which was about ten miles south. They were headed the right way in a roundabout way. The aqueduct road they took went up high and in and out several canyons before it came out at the north division fence of their winter range. I couldn't see them and I figured they had followed the creek down. As I eased down to the aqueduct looking for tracks, you could have knocked me over with a feather—up the hill on the road the tracks went. I peeked around the corner and they were plodding along single file going south. I said

to my horse. "You old wind-broke bugger, let's see what you can do." I eased up as close as I could, still a long run, and put the spurs to my horse. He tore up the ground, and after a short run, I had turned them down canyon again. Here, again, they surprised me. Instead of hitting the creek and following it down, they went straight across and started angling around the hill, turning north again.

My horse was "give out," so I just sat there and watched them go. About half a mile around, they stopped again and stood looking back. I figured this was my last chance to make them think I had given up on them, so in plain sight, I started back up the canyon. I had to take it slowly because Cho Cho was really huffing and puffing. That last run up hill just about did him in. What I had in mind was to go far enough up the canyon out of sight and run out on the left slope of the canyon quite a bit above them. I might turn them if they didn't take off again. When I thought I was above them and ahead of them, I peeked over the hill. This is all about a fifty percent slope of soft sand with a scattering of rocks, greasewood, and sagebrush. I was just a little ahead of them and about 500 yards above when they saw me. They started on the trot and I just kept a little ahead of them. Finally, they stopped and looked at me. I was close enough that they could hear me, so I started talking to them, "Easy, gal; easy, baby;" and all that good stuff. I gradually worked around in front of them, still a little above. They were as hot as my horse was by this time. A couple of the big calves (450 pounds) had their tongues out, which is what they do when they get too hot. By gently working them down hill, I got them in sight of the Nine Mile corral. I just held them there for about a half an hour while the stock got their wind back and the cows got to where they seemed to recognize me. By this time, my buddy, Walter, had the corral all ready, and started up my way. Was I glad to see him! As usual, Walt knew just where to position himself, and after a few short runs, we had them in the corral.

The corral at Nine Mile isn't even a good bluff. They could jump out any time they put their minds to it. We eased them up the chute, and with a little luck and a hot shot, jumped them in the truck. We now had nine cows and four big calves. This was really too many, but we had no choice, because if we split up our pairs (left a cow or calf behind), we didn't know when or where we would see them again. They were tight; so tight they couldn't wiggle. I noticed a couple of cows that had their heads up and a horn out below the top bar, and they had to stay in that uncomfortable position the whole one and one-half hour trip home. We stopped and checked a few times, but they were still in the same position.

Lorraine Bailey had come along just as we were loading and offered to haul our horses back to the ranch. She is one of the owners of the Smith Ranch and it would only be about twelve miles out of her way. We took her up on it because it had been a long day since I had started after the cattle in Nine Mile Canyon.

A long, drawn-out story to tell about running a few cows down the draw and getting them loaded, but I tell it with the hope that those who haven't worked cattle under these conditions might be able to understand how one might work cattle in this one situation. Someone else might have done it a little differently, and on another day, I might have, too. I'll probably say this so many times you will be tired of it, but you just have to "keep reading your cattle" and try to have a running plan that will keep you at least part-way in control. You do your best with what you have. Many times your horse is tired out by the time something like this comes up. You have to keep your eyes open and try to out-guess your stock; be ready to change your plan of operation at any time. I guess I'd say your best plan is to try to hold cattle like this up, if possible, until they quiet down a little. Keep your distance so they won't feel too threatened. The cattle we were working in this chapter were basically gentle range cattle who were on a strange range and hadn't had contact with people for a few weeks. I've seen my share of cattle right in the same canyon who would have just thrown their tails over their backs and left the country.

When we had loaded our cows and started back to the ranch, I was reminded of a happening with a wild heifer right below the same corral in Nine Mile Canyon some forty years earlier, and I told Walt about it as we drove home.

I think it was about 1945 when Marcus Rudnick turned some cattle out on the Smith Ranch range just for one spring. Marcus sent about five cowboys out to the Mojave Desert to gather his cattle and bring them back to the Kern River Valley. In the process of gathering the Rudnick cattle, we came across four or five "big ears" (animals who had left their mothers, were between one year and two years old, and did not have their ears marked). The range was that alloted to the Smith and Powers

ranches for their winter and spring range. Because the Rudnick cattle were all branded when they were turned out, we knew those unbranded animals we found belonged either to my Dad or to Stanley Smith. We proceeded to ear-mark them as we found them, and we would brand them the next time we got them to the home ranch. Some of these cattle hadn't seen a man for a year and were wild as deer. We had only 250 head of cows on the Powers Ranch, and I could usually remember if I had seen the young unbranded animal following one of my Dad's cows. I could also recognize those coming from the Smith stock. As we rode the country around the Nine Mile Corral, we came across a little bunch up high on the canyon hillside. There was a big two year old heifer in the bunch without a brand or earmark. I recognized her right away as one who had been on a cow of my Dad's. We started them down off the hill and they were going ninety miles an hour. I can't remember if I got a rope on the heifer or not, but she was stopped on the flat below the Nine Mile Corral with a rope around her head and one front foot. One of the cowboys picked up both hind feet and we stretched the heifer out on the ground. Because I knew the Powers earmark the best, I got off and trimmed both ears in the appropriate manner. When I finished, I took the rope off her head and had started back to my horse when I remembered that I had taken my gloves off to get my knife out and had left them laying on the ground. The heifer was still stretched out and didn't realize the rope was off her head. I looked at the man who had the heels and asked, "Do you still have her?" He nodded "yes," so I turned to walk back to the animal. Just as I got to her, I saw the heel rope slack, and almost that quick she got her feet under her and jumped up. Some might think she would run off into the sunset, but like any redblooded American cow, she tried to get friendly with me. I ran for my horse, but this scared him and he took off. I was on my own. The boys just sat around betting on who was the fastest, me or the heifer.

The flat below the Nine Mile Corral was covered with boulders about three to four feet around that had come down in a cloudburst in the 30's. The heifer being almost two years old, had nice little sharp horns about nine inches long. She was doing her best to poke some holes in me. I would run around one of the boulders and she would either run around the boulder after me or try to jump over. The crew were sitting around laughing their heads off. After a few minutes, she gave up and ran off down the canyon. I was pretty mad at the time, and as the man who had turned the heifer loose brought up my horse, I hollered at him, "I thought you said you had him." He didn't say a word, just sat there grinning. Before long, I also saw the humor in it and some forty years later, every time I pass that spot, I think how funny I must have looked trying to out-dodge that mad heifer in the boulder patch. We would all pull jokes like that on each other; some of them not too safe, but good entertainment.

# Index